# Leonard Cohen's
## *Book of Mercy*

# Leonard Cohen's *Book of Mercy*

An Interpretation

DORON B. COHEN

WIPF & STOCK · Eugene, Oregon

LEONARD COHEN'S *BOOK OF MERCY*
An Interpretation

Copyright © 2026 Doron B. Cohen. All rights reserved. Except for brief quotations in critical publications or reviews, no part of this book may be reproduced in any manner without prior written permission from the publisher. Write: Permissions, Wipf and Stock Publishers, 199 W. 8th Ave., Suite 3, Eugene, OR 97401.

Wipf & Stock
An Imprint of Wipf and Stock Publishers
199 W. 8th Ave., Suite 3
Eugene, OR 97401

www.wipfandstock.com

PAPERBACK ISBN: 978-1-6667-8931-7
HARDCOVER ISBN: 978-1-6667-8932-4
EBOOK ISBN: 978-1-6667-8933-1

VERSION NUMBER 01/07/26

The Hebrew Bible quoted mostly from the *Tanakh: The Holy Scripture* © The Jewish Publication Society of America, 1917. In Fair Use.

The New Testament quoted from the New International Version © Biblica, Inc. In Fair Use.

The Jewish Prayer Book quoted mostly from: *Siddur Tehilat Hashem, Nusach Ha-Ari Zal* © Merkos L'Inyonei Chinuch, 2013. In Fair Use.

*Sefer Ha-Zohar*: Excerpts from ZOHAR: THE BOOK OF SPLENDOR: BASIC READINGS FROM THE KABBALAH selected and edited by Gershom G. Scholem, copyright 1949 and copyright © renewed 1977 by Penguin Random House LLC. Used by permission of Schocken Books, an imprint of the Knopf Doubleday Publishing Group, a division of Penguin Random House LLC. All rights reserved.

Excerpts from THE BOOK OF MERCY by Leonard Cohen. Copyright © 1984 by Leonard Cohen, used by permission of The Wylie Agency (UK) Limited. Excerpts from THE SPICE-BOX EARTH by Leonard Cohen. Copyright © 1961 by Leonard Cohen, used by permission of The Wylie Agency (UK) Limited. Excerpts from STRANGER MUSIC by Leonard Cohen. Copyright © 1993, Leonard Cohen and Leonard Cohen Stranger Music, Inc. Excerpts from THE FAVORITE GAME by Leonard Cohen. Copyright © 2003, 1961 by Leonard Cohen, used by permission of The

Wylie Agency (UK) Limited. Excerpts from BOOK OF LONGING by Leonard Cohen. Copyright © 2006 by Leonard Cohen, used by permission of The Wylie Agency (UK) Limited. Song Lyrics "Suzanne", "Master Song", "The Stranger Song", "Sisters Of Mercy", "So Long Marianne", "Teachers", "Bird On A Wire", "Story Of Isaac", "Joan Of Arc", "The Gypsy Wife", "Dance Me to the End of Love", "Coming Back to You", "Hallelujah", "If It Be Your Will", "The Tower Of Song", "The Future", "Waiting For The Miracle", "Anthem", from STRANGER MUSIC by Leonard Cohen. Copyright © 1993, Leonard Cohen and Leonard Cohen Stranger Music, Inc., used by permission of The Wylie Agency (UK) Limited. Song Lyrics: "Stories Of The Street", 1967; "The Old Revolution", 1969; "Last Year's Man", 1971; "Please Don't Pass Me By", 1973; "Lover, Lover, Lover", 1974; "The Law", "Hunter's Lullaby", "Heart With No Companion", 1984; "Here It Is", "Boogie Street", 2001; "Amen", "Show Me The Place", "Come Healing", 2012; "Almost Like the Blues", "Born in Chains", 2014; "You Want It Darker", "Treaty", 2016; "It's Torn", 2019 by Leonard Cohen © used by permission of The Wylie Agency (UK) Limited.

# Contents

*Preface and Acknowledgments* | ix

Introduction | 1
  On the Writing of *Book of Mercy* | 3
  The Title and Structure of the Book | 9
  Major Themes | 12

Notes on the Individual Poems | 15
  I | 17
  II | 74
  Conclusion | 111

*Bibliography and Discography* | 113
  1. The Work of Leonard Cohen Referred to or Quoted | 113
  2. Jewish and Other Sources | 114
  3. Interviews, Biographies and Studies | 115

*The Work of Leonard Cohen Referred to or Quoted* | 117
*Ancient Document Index* | 119
*Subject Index* | 123
*Places Index* | 125
*Names Index* | 127
*A List of Key Words in the Book* | 129

# Preface and Acknowledgments

I BECAME FAMILIAR WITH Leonard Cohen's work during my early teens, and over the past decades have considered him an intimate companion mentally even though distant in every other sense. It took me a long while to feel ready to share this private intimacy with others, but in 2006 this changed as I joined the *Leonard Cohen Forum* on which I soon initiated an open discussion of *Book of Mercy*. The discussion lasted for three and a half years, sometimes going at breakneck pace, other times it seemed as if it were dying out, but we persevered in discussing the book from beginning to end. Dozens of participants from around the world took part, regularly or occasionally, and I benefited greatly from many of their contributions. This experience made it possible for me to fulfill an old dream by translating the book into Hebrew and adding a detailed commentary (the book was published in Jerusalem by Carmel, 2015, as *Sefer Rachamim*). Eventually I decided to rewrite and expand my commentary, this time in English, and offer it to those interested in Cohen's work and particularly in his book of prayers. I wish to use this occasion to thank a few of the participants in the Forum discussion whose contributions were of particular meaning for me, some of whom also assisted me in various ways as I was compiling my notes later on. Special thanks then are due to: Tomislav Sakic from Croatia, Sylvain Belisle from Canada, the poet Mathew Robert James from Australia, Joseph Way of the United States, and Judy Remy from France. I also wish

## Preface and Acknowledgments

to remember Greg Wells from the US, who passed away during the Forum discussion but not before making some unforgettable contributions to it including an index for the book, and the Canadian poet Judith Fitzgerald, who had a unique insight into the work of Leonard Cohen.

My deepest gratitude to Professor Louis Schwartz of the University of Richmond for his generosity in reading my manuscript and making a long list of corrections and suggestions, most of which I adopted. Thanks to his contribution, this work has been greatly improved and enhanced. I thanked him several times along my text for suggesting specific quotes, but he also helped me in myriad other ways for which I am most grateful.

When my Hebrew book was published, Leonard Cohen was still alive and I was able to thank him for everything, including his assistance in obtaining the rights for the translation. Now that he has passed away this current work is dedicated to his memory.

Kyoto
Concluded May 2018
Revised July 2023
Prepared for printing August 2025

# Introduction

LEONARD COHEN GAINED HIS universal fame mostly as a singer-songwriter, but his work was not limited to that single field alone. During a career lasting over sixty years he published, on top of his recorded albums and concerts, several poetry books and novels as well as graphic and video art. His work displayed an ongoing fascination with love and eroticism along with a constant and deep quest for ways of life and faith, while also dealing with fundamental social and political issues. During those long years of creativity Cohen produced a vast body of work in which various parts reflect each other, and to which he kept adding until the very final moments of his life. Amid his vast body of work *Book of Mercy* occupies a special place as a condensed expression of the spiritual aspects of its author's quest.

Cohen published *Book of Mercy* in 1984 as he turned fifty. It was his tenth book, following seven volumes of poetry and two novels, and his last original volume before a long hiatus which ended only in 2006, with the publication of *Book of Longing*, although in between a collection of selected poetry and song lyrics, *Stranger Music*, was published in 1993. Of all his books, *Book of Mercy* is arguably his most distinctly Jewish one, at least since his second volume of poetry, *The Spice-Box of Earth* (1961); it contains allusions to, and paraphrases of, verses from the Hebrew Bible and the *Siddur* (the Jewish Prayer Book), as well as the literature of the Midrash and the Kabbalah, and the teachings of Hasidism. Speaking on writing this book, Cohen said that part of the motivation was his wish "to affirm the traditions I had inherited."[1] Indeed, the book can be viewed as part of the long tradition of Jewish liturgy, and it may also reflect the spirit of Midrash which uses familiar verses to create a new meaning relevant for each age. Still, as can be expected, the book is "Jewish" in Cohen's unique terms, since it also contains some Christian imagery, as well as reflections of Zen Buddhism, which Cohen practiced for many long years. Simultaneously with this volume Cohen also released his eighth studio album, *Various Positions*, and close scrutiny will reveal many mutual reflections between the book and the album, as between the two halves of a diptych: listening to the songs on the album reveals much about the intention of the book and vice versa.

In the following notes I do not presume to offer a full or unequivocal interpretation of the book. My reading of it is not the only possible one, and other readers will undoubtedly find in it different meanings. However, based on many years of studying it, I thought I might offer certain notes and explanations as an aid to readers in understanding this far from simple book. My goal in writing these notes is threefold. Firstly, I aim to identify the literary sources which left their mark on the book's language. Although Cohen never specified his sources, it is often possible to identify certain biblical and liturgical verses quoted or paraphrased by him, the Midrash, Kabbalah, and Hasidism's teachings that inspired him, and also the Zen traditions and practices reflected in the book. Secondly, I aim to offer possible interpretations of some of the images that are essential to the book's fabric, based on the study of Cohen's vast body of work in poetry, songs, prose, and graphic art, referring to specific works and quoting from them. Finally, I will offer a selection of cross-references between the book's poems that I hope might help the reader to better understand the meaning of the text and deepen the reading experience (I will also cross-reference my notes in order to avoid frequent repetitions). In fact, I engage here only with some of the questions raised by Cohen's text, by its modes of expression and the allusions and echoes

1. Nadel, *Various Positions*, 238.

INTRODUCTION

I have been able to identify, but to follow the Jewish dictum, the gates of interpretation are never sealed, and other readers may find their own path in reading Cohen's challenging book and offer further insights into it. I should perhaps also clarify at the outset that personally I do not fully share Cohen's religious sensibilities, but I am drawn by his use of language, by his weaving of various traditions into the one to which he was committed, and by the somewhat enigmatic nature of his work, all of which motivate me to try to understand it better.

## ON THE WRITING OF *BOOK OF MERCY*

As noted above, *Book of Mercy* was published in the same year as its author's fiftieth birthday, and for that reason, presumably, it contains exactly fifty poems. The fiftieth year is Jubilee, the year in which, among other things, slaves are to go free (Lev 25:8–17), and this undoubtedly had a special meaning for Cohen, who hoped (but failed) to be released from his enslavement to the depression he suffered most of his adult life.[2] Years later, in the song "Treaty" on the album *You Want It Darker* released shortly before his death, Cohen sings: "They're dancing in the street—it's Jubilee / We sold ourselves for love but now we're free." More about his depression is said later on, but it may be construed that at the time of publishing his book Cohen could only hope for the liberation that he seems to have achieved only two decades later.

The book was written in a relatively short period, and was published soon afterwards. By that time, Cohen had separated from his partner Suzanne Elrod, the mother of his son Adam (born 1972) and daughter Lorca (born 1974). Suzanne and the children had relocated to the village Bonnieux in Provence, southern France, and Cohen would go visit them, staying in a trailer parked in a field outside the family's home.[3] The place, conditions, and family relations are reflected in some of the book's poems,

---

2. Simmons, *I'm Your Man*, 57 and passim.
3. Simmons, *I'm Your Man*, 310; Nadel, *Various Positions*, 230.

and although in principle the book should be interpreted based on internal evidence, it is hard and sometimes impossible to ignore its author's circumstances. However, in the following notes I distinguish between "the speaker," the voice heard in the text, and "Cohen," when quoting from his other work or referring to biographical data.

During the said period and previous years, Cohen, who never cut off his Jewish roots and was proud of his belonging to a priestly family, intensified his immersion in Jewish literature and custom.[4] As a child, apart from regular schooling, he attended Hebrew School (thrice weekly between the ages of seven and fourteen, according to his testimony), and frequented the *Shaar Hashomayim* Synagogue in Montreal, of which his family was one of the main pillars for several generations. His maternal grandfather, Rabbi Solomon Klonitzki-Kline, lived in the family house for a year when Cohen was a university student and used to study the Book of Isaiah with him.[5] Although he continued studying during his adult years, his command of Hebrew was limited (although probably above average among North American Jews), and he used a bilingual *Siddur* and English translations of Talmudic and Kabbalistic texts. Still, in spite of his immersion in religious texts it cannot be said that Cohen wrote his book based on systematic theological reflections, but rather on a poet's intuition. Jewish Mysticism scholar Elliot R. Wolfson argued that Cohen had deep insights into the Kabbalah, partially reached "unwittingly,"[6] but even if Wolfson is correct this does not make Cohen a theologian or a Kabbalist. Be that as it may, during his childhood and later life Cohen undoubtedly absorbed much of the language and spirit of the Jewish sources, both of which underwent certain transformations in the poet's internal laboratory, and were expressed poignantly in his poetry, and in particular in *Book of Mercy*. Hebrew expressions

---

4. Benazon, "Leonard Cohen of Montreal," 53; Kurzweil, "I *Am* the Little Jew Who Wrote the Bible," 384.

5. Benazon, "Leonard Cohen of Montreal," 52.

6. Wolfson, "New Jerusalem Glowing," 143. See also my comment, D.B. Cohen, "Speaking Sweetly from 'The Window,'" 119–20.

# Introduction

then, are often in the background, although it should always be remembered that Cohen's creative tool was the English language in all its richness.

Apart from his Jewish education Cohen was influenced by other traditions. During his childhood he had a Catholic nanny, and the Christian environment in Montreal where he was born and grew up left a lasting mark on his work. The figure of Jesus became particularly meaningful for him, often appearing in his poetry in name or in indirect allusions. Cohen explained on several occasions that for him Jesus existed apart from the organized Church, taking part in all human experience, and therefore, although never considering conversion, Cohen continually referred to Jesus as a figure full of grace. The inclusion of Jesus in his work also helped open it to a wider audience unfamiliar with the Jewish sources.

In 1969 Cohen made the acquaintance of the Zen master Joshu Sasaki Roshi, and started practicing Zen meditation under his guidance. Sasaki was born in Japan in 1907, went to America, where he opened several Zen centers, in 1962, and was active until his death in 2014, aged 107. Cohen would always refer to him simply as "Roshi," the honorific title for venerated Zen masters. By the time he was composing *Book of Mercy* Cohen had already accumulated considerable experience in Zen, having stayed for longer or shorter periods of meditation and study in the monasteries and Zen centers headed by his master, who also became a friend. During the 1990's, a decade after the publication of the book, Cohen was to spend about five years in the monastery on Mount Baldy outside Los Angeles. After leaving the monastery Cohen also spent long periods in India, studying with the Hindu master Ramesh S. Balsekar, whom he considered another important teacher.[7]

Cohen did not regard Zen Buddhism in terms of religion. On one of the many occasions on which he was asked about it he explained: "Buddhist meditation frees you from God and frees you from religion. You can experience complete at-homeness in this world."[8] On another occasion he said of Zen: "as I received it

---

7. Simmons, *I'm Your Man*, 394–403.
8. Turner, "Leonard Cohen: The Profits of Doom," 211.

from my teacher, there is no conflict [with Judaism] because there is no prayerful worship and there is no discussion of a deity."[9] Cohen also explained that the messianic meaning of Judaism for him was, on the one hand to be loyal to the Jewish tradition, and on the other hand the belief that "we all are part of a brotherhood under the Almighty," and therefore there is no justification for the exclusiveness and scorn of other nations displayed by some Jews.[10] These ideas are also expressed in *Book of Mercy*.

Concerning the writing of the book Cohen said: "I began to have the courage to write down my prayers. To apply to the source of mercy . . . I found that the act of writing was the proper form for my prayer. It was the only type of sound I could make."[11] He added that the book came "from an intense desire to speak in that way . . . And you don't speak in that way unless you feel truly cornered, unless you feel truly desperate and you feel urgency in your life . . ."[12] Still, such feelings were not new for Cohen, neither was this style of writing. In his long prose-poem "Lines from my Grandfather's Journal" in his second collections of poems, he expressed the following notion: "Prayer makes speech a ceremony. To observe this ritual in the absence of arks, altars, a listening sky: this is a rich discipline."[13] Moreover, a "prayer" reminiscent of those in *Book of Mercy* can already be found in his first novel, *The Favourite Game*, beginning with the following lines (which quote Isa 6:3, a verse incorporated into the daily prayer, as elaborated on later):

> Friday night. Sabbath. Ritual music on the PA. Holy, holy, holy Lord God of Hosts. The earth is full of your glory. If I could only end my hate. If I could believe what they wrote and wrapped in silk and crowned with gold. I want to write the word.[14]

9. Kurzweil, "I *Am* the Little Jew Who Wrote the Bible," 375.
10. Kurzweil, "I *Am* the Little Jew Who Wrote the Bible," 379.
11. Twigg, "Leonard Cohen," 46.
12. Nadel, *Various Positions*, 238.
13. Cohen, *The Spice-Box of Earth*, 82.
14. Cohen, *The Favourite Game*, 194.

INTRODUCTION

However, long years of experience and mental struggle, of reading and writing, found their crystallization in *Book of Mercy*. Cohen elaborated further on the book in a radio interview in Canada the year the book was published, saying, among other points:

> Those kind of questions, 'I believe' or 'I don't believe', those belong to the mind, and appropriately to the mind, but, you know, like they say 'there's no atheist in the foxhole'. When you find yourself in that landscape where the only thing you can do is prayer, it doesn't matter whether you believe or not, because you're not using this faculty that evaluates the reality of faith or the reality of God or not, it's a completely different landscape. It is a cry, and there is an object of the cry, and it's a certainty in that place . . . One is not interested in proving or in not proving the existence of the object . . . If you address yourself to the source of mercy, and you might have the good luck to discover that there is a source of mercy, that doesn't turn you into an evangelist or . . . and it doesn't serve an argument, it's not theology. There **is** a source of mercy, as I experienced it, and these poems are the document of that address and that kind of deliverance.[15]

Cohen was deeply influenced by various literary-mystical traditions including Islamic Sufi poetry, and there are those who regard him as a mystic who may even have had the wish to unite with a divine entity and be absorbed by it. In my view, careful reading of his poems does not reveal such a tendency. Although his work turns towards the absolute, it maintains a constant allegiance to the transient. In the poem "I Have Not Lingered in European Monasteries" in *The Spice-Box of Earth* Cohen says: "I have not held my breath / so that I might hear the breathing of God, / or tamed my heartbeat with an exercise, / or starved for visions."[16] Although things might have changed for him later, due among other elements to his Zen experience, he never tried to cross all boundaries or disassociate himself from any aspect of the physical world, base or profound. This is also in line with the tradition of Jewish esotericism including

---

15. Gzowsky, "Leonard Cohen at 50".
16. Cohen, *The Spice-Box of Earth*, 21.

the Kabbalah. The majority of Kabbalah practitioners wished to discover the mysteries of creation, the inner structure of the Godhead and its activity in the world, and to understand human beings' role in creation and the meaning of the commandments that must be fulfilled, rather than aspire to being absorbed by the divine, a wish more typical to Christian mystics. The more common wish of Jewish mystics is to mend the current world on the path to full redemption. Similarly, Cohen never claimed to have gained "enlightenment" (*satori*) in his Zen experience. His approach to religion was poetical, in both inspiration and output, although he was also seeking its therapeutic aspects.

It should also be pointed out that "love" for Cohen is always directed both upwards and downwards: the religious urge is not separated from the sexual drive or emotional energy. It is often hard to decide whether he is talking to a hidden divine entity or a visible feminine one, and some of his poems can be interpreted both ways, which must have been his intention. Also, the speaker in his poems is never released from his pain; he prays for it, as he does constantly in *Book of Mercy*, but apparently never reaching his goal. He lives in a broken reality, and although continually trying to mend it, he never quite succeeds. Cohen tried many remedies for his depression, from medicine, drugs, and alcohol to sex and religion. According to him, nothing helped, but when he was around sixty five years old he realized, to his own great surprise, that he was no longer depressed without knowing quite why, although the long years of training with Roshi and the shorter period with Balsekar may have helped.[17] Undoubtedly, praying was an expression of a mental need in an attempt to be released from depression and despair, a fact that stands out all through the book, although there must have been other motivations as well.

Cohen also said of the book: "It is that curious thing: a private book that has a public possibility. But it's not my intention to become known as a writer of prayers."[18] The private and the public indeed come together in this little book, which can convey various

---

17. Simmons, *I'm Your Man*, 402.
18. Sward, "An interview with Leonard Cohen," 167.

meanings for different people, although close scrutiny of the language used in it can clarify the intended meaning in most cases. It has no doubt resonated around the world, having been republished in at least five editions from 1984 to 2019, and translated into more than a dozen languages, including French, Spanish, Italian, German, Swedish, Danish, Finish, Czech, Slovenian, Croatian, Polish, Greek and Hebrew, some in two different translations.

## THE TITLE AND STRUCTURE OF THE BOOK

Cohen deliberated with himself for a long time in choosing the right title for his book. During the editing process the book was alternatively titled "The Name" and "The Shield," words repeated frequently in it. The word "god" appears only three times in the whole book (twice capitalized), but "the name" (*Ha-Shem* in Hebrew, the substitute for uttering God's holy name YHWH, which is taboo for observant Jews) appears dozens of times, occasionally capitalized. "Shield" can refer to "David's Shield" (*Magen David* as it is known in Jewish tradition), and indeed the book's cover is adorned with the symbol envisioned by Cohen (and designed for the cover by Michael van Elsen), which later became closely identified with him. It is a Star of David made up of two combined hearts, symbolizing the wish for unity. Cohen used to refer to it as the symbol of "the Order of the Unified Heart." After long deliberations, Cohen opted for *Book of Mercy*, without the definite article, so as not to presume to be offering *the* book on the subject, but more modestly, one of many possible books.[19] This choice was also followed years later in the title of *Book of Longing*. Intentionally or not, Cohen followed a Hebrew tradition (not a consistent one, admittedly) of titles containing the word "book" followed by a noun without the definite article, such as *Sefer Yetzirah* (Book of Creation), an early work of Jewish esotericism.

The word "mercy" appears in many of Cohen's songs, beginning with "Sisters Of Mercy" on *Songs of Leonard Cohen*, his first

---

19. Simmons, *I'm Your Man*, 314.

album, and including other songs which will be mentioned later on. The book's title can be interpreted in several ways: a book addressing mercy, offering mercy, belonging to an entity called "Mercy," and more. The Hebrew equivalent, *rachamim*, appears in many of the biblical verses and liturgical expressions alluded to in the book. In the Kabbalah, it is one of the titles of the sixth of the ten *sefirot* (singular *sefirah*) or emanations, known mostly as *Tif'eret* (Beauty). *Tif'eret* is the *sefirah* which balances the powers of grace and judgment, and also represents the male aspect, opposite *Malchut* (Kingdom), which represents the female one; their union is expressed in the Aramaic verse translated as "The unification of the Holy One, blessed be He, and his Presence," which became an opening formula of some prayers and appears in most versions of the *Siddur*. *Book of Mercy* includes many allusions to the *sefirot* as will be shown in the following notes.

It should be pointed out that in some traditions "mercy" is associated with a female figure, such as Mary the mother of Jesus in Catholicism. In the Buddhist tradition there is a figure which gradually assumed the position of a goddess of mercy: Kannon (in its Japanese version) or Gwan Yin (the Chinese one). Originally it was the bodhisattva *Avalokiteśvara*, a figure which gradually changed from a male to a female figure during the passage of the tradition connected with him from India through China, Korea and Japan. Cohen's book expresses yearning for various female figures, but the identity of the "you" spoken to is sometimes ambiguous.

Following the title page there appears a dedication, "for my teacher." It is commonly assumed that the dedication is to Roshi, the person who was Cohen's principle teacher at the time and in the following years, and who often appeared in his poetry (see notes to poems 1, 2 and 21). But there were several other important figures in Cohen's life whom he regarded as his teachers, particularly from among the Montreal poets whom he came to know in his younger years. In his second poetry book Cohen wrote poems about some of them and dedicated poems to others, among them "To a Teacher," dedicated to F. R. Scott, "Last Dance at the Four

## Introduction

Penny" depicting Irving Layton, and "Song for Abraham Klein" for A. M. Klein.[20] The first of these three poems is recited on the *Dear Heather* album, which also includes Cohen's reciting of Scott's poem "Villanelle for Our Time." There is also the song "Teachers" on Cohen's first album, expressing his complex feelings towards such figures.

The book is divided into two uneven parts and fifty numbered prose-poems, some very short with only a few lines, and some somewhat or considerably longer (but none longer than a page and a half). They are not printed like poems in short lines, but their poetic qualities stand out, and some could be arranged in stanzas. Although they are best defined as "prose poems," for the sake of convenience they are referred to here as "poems." Cohen himself usually referred to them as "prayers" (and occasionally as "poems"), although not every poem reads as a distinct prayer. Some indeed sound like prayers from a suffering heart, along the model of the "individual lament" in the Book of Psalms, in which the speaker complains of physical or mental anguish, asking for God's help and certain of being heard (for example, poems 5, 6, 7, 12, 28, 31, and 37 in the book; see Pss 3, 5, 6, 7, and so on). Other poems follow the model of the "hymn," psalms which glorify God's greatness and praise his care for the world (poems 9, 14, 29, 39, and 43 among others; compare Pss 8, 19, 29, and others), or that of "individual thanksgiving" for salvation (poems 10, 19, and 34; Pss 9, 10, 18, 23, 30, 34, 40, and others). However, in most cases Cohen did not follow the biblical model to the letter, but combined several psalmic forms in one poem. Also, as he often did in his earlier poetry, some poems seem to report an incident in the speaker's physical or mental life, which is given a literary-poetic guise (poems 1, 2, 3, 4, 11, and others), while a few are written as short stories or parables with a double meaning (18, 23, and 25). A few poems include political, social or environmental concerns, using the admonishing tone of biblical prophecy (27 and 30).

Cohen, therefore, brings together in this book various generic forms used in his previous writing, including the lyric poem,

---

20. Cohen, *The Spice-Box of Earth*, 20; 64–65; 66.

various forms of prose narrative, and various forms of prayer (petitional, confessional, and doxological). Like his other works, the book also reflects various major issues and events in the author's life. The language, as will be seen, mostly originates in the Jewish tradition. The book's spirit expresses crisis and loss, but simultaneously confidence that there is a source of mercy that the speaker can address with his prayers. As Cohen indicated, it is a very personal book, stemming from its author's experience, but it may also give expression to any person's feelings, which is the way of Jewish liturgy, from the Psalms to the present day.

## MAJOR THEMES

The book offers many themes, depicted in numerous variations. The main theme presented by the speaker is of being lost, feeling sinful and depressed. There are two paths that he implicitly tries to pursue: the Jewish tradition and the Way of Zen, but both present obstacles. In the case of the former, there are those, including occasionally the speaker himself, who follow the tradition out of habit despite it having lost any true meaning for them. As for the latter, the Way of Zen can be absurd and distressing, leading nowhere. Still, the speaker persists with both, although when the community fails him he turns his feeling, wishes, heart, and love towards "you" or "mercy" as the source for his deliverance.

The divine presence in the world is the major reassurance for the speaker. Although he rarely uses "God," preferring "the name" or just "you," the speaker finds this presence all around, manifesting itself in creation. It follows for him that the world does not belong to human beings, who are only temporary dwellers in it, but their disregard or unawareness of this fact raises prophetic rage in the speaker. He denounces injustice, condemns the actions of states, the validity of ideologies, and even the sincerity of protest, and decries environmental damage.

A subject that occurs often in the book, especially in part I, is the study of the Torah or the Law. The speaker encounters various difficulties in his quest to learn and understand more: the lack of

## Introduction

a partner, the difficulty of the text, and his own sinful and impure state which keeps the Torah, a text he occasionally personifies, at a distance from him, hidden by many obstacles. Still, he persists in his efforts. He wishes to follow the Law which does not stand in contrast or opposition to Mercy: both are objects of the speakers' desire.

As already noted above, the world of the speaker is a broken one. This brokenness is both personal in the speaker's life, and universal, and as such is connected with the notions of Lurianic Kabbalah according to which the state of brokenness is inherent to the world and requires mending (see notes for poem 1 below). Consequently, the speaker seeks the mending of both levels, although he realizes that this would be a messianic reality that could be imagined but probably not fulfilled.

The book approaches the subject of the family in various aspects: the speaker's deceased parents, to whom he feels strongly attached; his children, for the future of whom he is worried; his partner, who is elusive and not clearly defined; and families on a larger scale, such as the Jewish people or humanity as a whole, to both of which he harbors both attachment and distaste.

As far as the female partner is concerned, there is a marked difference between the current book and Cohen's previous one, *Death of a Lady's Man* (1978), which was, in part, an angry diatribe against the speaker's female companion. Here the feelings and language are much more subdued. The erotic aspect is also more subtly and indirectly expressed than in much of the rest of Cohen's work.

Another important subject is the speaker's creativity, expressed in writing and in song. Concerning his work and his personality in general, he vacillates between arrogance, which causes him to feel sinful, and humility, which drives him to ask for mercy. Still, he expresses continuous commitment to his work in spite of the considerable obstacles he must surmount.

The poems are independent, but a certain narrative arch and certain stylistic structure may also be discerned across the book. The narrative begins with the failure of reconnecting with the tradition; gradually this reconnection is happening, but never unequivocally: a certain peak in poems 5 and 6 is followed by stumbling and falling in poems 7 and 8. The vacillation between hope and despair continues, and a climax of sort is reached in poem 15. Doubts, failure and pain are articulated also in many poems of the second part of the book, but the tone becomes gradually more reconciliatory. Poem 48 may constitute another climax, bringing together many of the motifs sounded along the book, but again this and the following last two poems do not proclaim a victory, only a certain hope. Stylistically, the first part (poems 1 to 26) has more poems of the "episode" or "parable" kinds, and fewer distinct prayers. The second part (poems 27 to 50) opens in the prophetic style of condemnation, but the great majority of its poems are distinct prayers, and it is largely more lyrical, expressing the speaker's emotional state rather than his physical reality.

# Notes on the Individual Poems

# I

THE FIRST PART OF the book comprises twenty-six of its fifty poems. The asymmetrical division could be the influence of the spirit of Zen. See Part II below for another possible explanation.

**1**

The book opens with the sense of loss. An anticipated meeting has not taken place, and years spent in idleness and ignorance haven't helped. Something must be done. An effort leads to the understanding that reality is broken, symbolized by the fact that the king is away from his throne. The archetype of the vacant throne on which the deserving king is not sitting is a universal one, but in the Jewish context it has several specific meanings: the Messiah king who is designed to sit on his throne at the future fulfilment of redemption; the exile of the *Shechinah*, God's presence, which has been wandering the world since the destruction of the Jerusalem temple, God's earthly throne; and the Kabbalistic meaning, of which there is more than one. In the classic Kabbalah, that of *Sefer ha-Zohar* (*Book of Splendor*), created mostly in thirteenth century Spain, the fissure in the universe is symbolized in the disrupted connection between the two *sefirot* respectively representing the male and female elements, *Tif'eret* ("Beauty," and also "Mercy") and *Malchut* ("Kingdom," the *Shechinah*), which severs the flow of divine vitality into the higher and lower worlds. Acccording to the Kabbalah, the ten *sefirot* are the expressions of divine revelation intellectually perceivable to human beings, who however may not perceive *Ein Sof*, the Infinite, the source of emanation. In the balanced condition the "king" is back on his "Throne of Glory" (*kise hakavod*). Among other symbolic ideas, the four lowest *sefirot* were described as the "four legs of the throne."

According to the Lurianic Kabbalah, developed in Safed in the sixteenth century under the leadership of Isaac Luria (known also as *Ha'Ari*), the current reality is the result of a catastrophic event in the Godhead during the "contraction," when the all-engulfing God contracted inwardly in order to leave a space for creation. However, the vessels that were to contain the divine light emanating into the vacant space broke under its potency, and sparks of light fell into the material world. Both the divine and created worlds are abject and broken, anticipating *tikkun*, the mending process through which the sparks will revert to their source, a process in which human beings have an important part to play. Several passages in *Book of Mercy* reveal that its author was influenced by the ideas of Lurianic Kabbalah, and the speaker in it is searching for ways of mending his broken world. From the point of view of the speaker in the first poem, although his efforts are insufficient (he can offer only buttons for love), a certain process of mending does begin during which he is returned to his childhood experience of the communal synagogue prayer. The speaker describes himself as a singer with a limited vocal range, but the experience of singing returns him to his right place in the community. Liturgy and secular singing become a unified voice.

Cohen often made connections between his studies of the Kabbalah and his experience in Zen Buddhism. Answering a question by Prof. Elliot R. Wolfson during a rare 2001 online chat on whether he studied the works of Kabbalah and Hasidism and was influenced by them, Cohen replied:

> I have a very superficial knowledge of the matter but even by dipping into the many books, I have been deeply touched by what I read, and by my conversations with

# I

living Hasidic masters. The model of the Tree of Life and the activities and interactions of the sephirot has been especially influential. The idea of the in-breath to clear a space for the whole manifestation and the out-breath as the place of the manifestation, has of course been illumined by my studies with Roshi and his instructions in zen meditation.[21]

As will be shown below, Kabbalah and Zen offer possible interpretations, not mutually exclusive, of various passages in the current and other poems.

As pointed out above, there are many shared reflections between the book and the album which was released the same year, *Various Positions* (abbreviated below as *VP*). For example, the king's throne is mentioned in "Hallelujah" ("She broke your throne, and she cut your hair"), and the same song mentions King David, who will reappear along the book and who the speaker identifies with. Further examples will be mentioned below.

In spite of the obvious Jewish content of this poem, it may also be read as a reflection of the experience at a Zen monastery, where the monks and novices gather early in the morning for meditation and chanting from the sutras. In this reading **"he"** would be Roshi, the venerated master, whose entrance everyone is awaiting (see also the following poem). In the poem "Roshi At 89,"[22] the master is depicted as "sitting in the throne-room," which in this case—in the spirit of Zen—could also be the toilet. Cohen told an interviewer concerning his relationship with Roshi:

> I've no interest in Zen Buddhism. I've no interest in Buddhism. If Roshi had been a professor of Astrophysics at Heidelberg I would have learned German and studied Astrophysics. I was interested in the man and I still am. That's what brought me to study Zen; it was that he manifested something that was beautiful to me. I wanted to study it.[23]

---

21. Wolfson, "New Jerusalem Glowing," 104.
22. Cohen, *Book of Longing*, 4.
23. Benazon, "Leonard Cohen of Montreal," 54.

On other occasions Cohen said that he was attracted to Zen mostly because of the practice and discipline, and not because of the contents. Monastic life was somewhat like military life, to which Cohen had been attracted since childhood.[24] However, long years spent practicing in the company of Zen monks undoubtedly had an impact on Cohen's ways of expression and world view.

**"I stopped to listen"**—The first step in the process of study and quest is listening. Years later Cohen would write in the song "Amen" on the album *Old Ideas*: "We're alone & I'm listening / I'm listening so hard that it hurts." The speaker stops whatever he is doing in order to study, reflect and start the process of mending.

**"I beg for mercy. Slowly he yields. Haltingly he moves toward his throne"**—In the background here, apart from the verses from Isaiah and the liturgy mentioned below, one can hear the verse from the *Selichot*, the penitential hymns and prayers recited in the period before and during the Jewish High Holidays and on other special occasions: "Almighty king, who sits on the throne of mercy, acting with benevolence." This line is meaningful not only for the first poem but for the whole book, in which the speaker turns time and again to "mercy," a word which appears in the book forty times, mentioned once or more in one half of its fifty poems. Another verse common in Jewish liturgy implores God: "Rise from the throne of judgment and sit on the throne of mercy." The throne also has an important place in Jewish esoteric writing since its earliest days in the genres known as *Heichalot* ("palaces") and *Merkava* ("chariot"), and throughout the various schools of Kabbalah, as mentioned above (and see also the notes for poem 44).

The Kabbalistic image of the throne was deeply imbedded in Cohen's mind; during his 1972 concert in Jerusalem, when he faced a mental difficulty that caused him to walk off the stage, he told the audience, among other things: "It says in the Kabbalah that unless Adam and Eve face each other, God does not sit on his throne."[25]

---

24. Nadel, *Various Positions*, 272.
25. Simmons, *I'm your Man*, 263.

# I

**"Reluctantly the angels grant to one another permission to sing"**—This is based on verses from the *Shema* part of the daily morning prayer:

> Praised be your Name, our King, who creates ministering angels, and whose ministering angels all stand in the highest of the universe and proclaim in awe, aloud in unison, the words of the living God and sovereign of the universe . . . They all take upon themselves the yoke of heavenly kingship, one from the other, and with love grant permission to each other to sanctify their maker with joyous spirit, with pure speech and sacred melody . . .

In the speaker's experience the angels are still giving each other permission "reluctantly" rather than "with love." The angels chant the *Kedusha*, or "Holiness verse," from Isa 6:3: "Holy, holy, holy, is the Lord of hosts; the whole earth is full of His glory," a verse quoted in various daily prayers. The same chapter in Isaiah opens with the vision of God "sitting upon a throne high and lifted up, and His train filled the temple." Undoubtedly, the current poem, with which Cohen chose to open his book, and much of the rest of it, reflect the synagogue liturgy absorbed by Cohen over the years, and his study of the Hebrew Bible with his grandfather.

"**. . . golden symmetry**"—This expression is not common in Jewish sources and sounds original and poetic, although in the background might be the "golden ratio," associated, among other things, with famous architectural monuments, and here refers to "the court." It may also refer to the system of the ten *sefirot*, which are arranged symmetrically.

"**. . . the lower choirs**"—The "Holiness verse" appears, among other prayers, in the *Musaf* prayer for Saturday and holidays, which is relevant to the book in various ways:

> A crown is given to you, Lord our God, by the angels, the supernal multitudes, and by your people Israel who assemble below. All of them together thrice repeat "holy" unto you, as it is written by your prophet: and they call

one another and say, holy, holy, holy, is the Lord of hosts;
the whole earth is full of His glory...

The speaker regains his place among those "assembled below" at the synagogue and who form "the lower choirs," who praise God together with the higher ones of the angels. Years later Cohen would remember his childhood experience vividly: "There was a whole *string* of Cohens standing up there in the front line singing our hearts out."[26] For the crown, mentioned at the beginning of the quoted passage, see poem 5.

"**. . . a singer**"—Cohen often said that he found it difficult to regard himself as a singer, and that he ventured on a singing career with great trepidation and for want of other choices. He was already thirty-three years old when he recorded his first album. He often joked about his limited vocal ability, as in "Tower of Song" on the album *I'm Your Man*: "I was born like this, I had no choice / I was born with the gift of a golden voice." From a different perspective there is the song "A Singer Must Die" on the album *New Skin for the Old Melody*; see also the poem "You'd Sing Too" in *Book of Longing*,[27] and poem 10.

2

This poem deals, among other things, with the speaker's feeling of distance from the Jewish tradition, and alternatively from the practice of Zen meditation, and of emerging from the protection of the community into a solitary world (**"When I left the king"**). The poem refers also to the speaker's difficulties as a creative personality, looking for ways to express himself to the world and having to face failures that injure his inflated ego.

"**. . . the king**"—Here, as in the first poem—in which he is not mentioned literally but only as "he" and associatively through the throne—the image of the king may refer to the divinity, but throughout the book the image also suggests the very human King

---

26. Benazon, "Leonard Cohen of Montreal," 51.
27. Cohen, *Book of Longing*, 6.

# I

David, the tormented sinner who is also the poet of the Psalms (for a different human identification, see below). The speaker identifies with David, like him feeling the burden of sin, aching for forgiveness and mercy, and like him wishing to sing of and praise God's glory and grace (see poem 7). It is possible, therefore, to interpret the reluctant and hesitant movement of "he" in the first poem, which eventually leads to the speaker's return to the protective community, also as a description of a process occurring within the speaker's own soul. In this and in subsequent poems it turns out, however, that the return does not lead to an unequivocal healing. The suffering and struggling are to last much longer (see also poem 48).

". . . **long rehearsals full of revisions**"—Cohen was known for his countless rewrites. The composition of a certain song could spread over several years, even decades, before a satisfying version would emerge, and even then he would often change words and lines when singing his songs in public. The two novels he published also underwent numerous rewrites, and two or three others never got published. Every recording or tour would entail laborious rehearsals.

". . . **the ape**"—This creature is born of the speaker's ambition, and there are several ways of interpreting its meaning. One possibility is that the ape represents Cohen's creative persona. This persona wavers between feeling alternatively grandiose and insignificant, partially due to unsuccessfully combating depression. In this case the creative persona is represented by an old and lazy ape. Some twenty five years later Cohen was to describe himself as "a lazy bastard living in a suit" in the song "Going Home" on the album *Old Ideas*.

In Jewish terms this symbol may refer to the notion of the "evil inclination" and its opposite "good inclination," both of which are essential parts of the human psyche and necessary for human existence since the "evil inclination" is also responsible for the creative and sexual drives, but it must be restrained. Here it is possible to view the ape as the "evil inclination" gone wild (see also the notes for poems 4 and 39). In "Master Song" on Cohen's first album is found "an ape with angel glands," who is making music on rubber bands, suggesting the combination of purity and bestiality, a motif not uncommon with Cohen.

Also may be relevant here is the Buddhist term "monkey mind" which signifies among other meanings being restless, capricious, confused, uncontrollable, and so on. Among its various usages in explaining psychological states, the term is commonly used in Zen practice to signify the difficulty in focusing on meditation, while the mind, which is easily distracted and keeps pulling in all directions, is like a monkey jumping from branch to branch. Another obstacle is the imitative nature of the monkey (see more below).

"*. . . the swept courtyards of the king*"—See "with broom and rag" in poem 44; in both cases the life in a Zen monastery could be implied (and see below).

"**'Bring me your ape'**"—The Zen Buddhist association stands out here more clearly than in the first poem. This sentence alludes to one of the fundamental Zen stories which exists in several versions. According to Zen tradition, the Indian monk Bodhidharma brought his teachings over to China in the sixth century CE ("Zen" is a Japanese word, based on the Chinese "Chan," in turn coming from the Sanskrit "Dhyana," meaning "meditation"). Before returning to India he appointed his disciple Dazu Huike (Taiso Eka in the Japanese version) as patriarch of the school; one of the exchanges between the master Bodhidharma and his disciple went as follows (in one of its several versions):

> "My soul is not yet pacified. Pray, Master, pacify it."
> "Bring me your soul, and I will have it pacified."
> "I have sought it these many years, and am still unable to get hold of it."
> "There! It is pacified once for all."[28]

The ape in Cohen's version might symbolize the soul or the mind in the original story, expressing the inner reluctance that

---

28. Suzuki, *Zen Buddhism*, 65. In other versions "soul" is substituted for "mind".

# I

often rises against the demands of practice and study, as does the monkey in the above-mentioned Buddhist expression. The ape asks dismissive questions for which the speaker has no answers, and he is disappointed by his master's reluctance to supply him with answers, since he must find them himself. This is also one of many examples of the creative and poetic use Cohen makes of his sources, crafting his own personal version of well-known material rather than quoting it directly (the ape is again mentioned in poems 20 and 22).

The association with Zen is also clarified by the prose piece titled "The End of My Life in Art" in Cohen's book *Death of a Lady's Man*, which was retitled "Roshi Again" in the collection *Stranger Music*; in particular it clarifies the present poem's line: **"He clowns behind his bars, imitating our hands in the dream."** This piece indeed reads like a report of a dream (or dreams) containing material from the daily sessions the Zen master holds with each novice, and in which Roshi is playing a guitar imitating his disciple's hand movements:

> I saw Roshi early this morning. His room was warm and fragrant. Soon he was hanging from a branch by his teeth. That made me laugh. But I didn't want to laugh. Then he was playing my guitar. From above he looked old and tired. From below he looked fresh and strong. Destroy particular self and absolute appears. He spoke to me gently. I waited for the rebuke. It didn't come. I waited because there is a rebuke in every other voice but his. He rang his bell. I bowed and left.
>
> I visited him again after several disagreeable hours in the mirror. He hung from the branch again. He looked down fearfully. He was afraid of falling. He was afraid of dying. He was depending on the branch and on his teeth. This is the particular self. This is the particular trance. He played my guitar. He copied my own fingering. He invented someone to interrupt him. He demonstrated the particular trance being broken by the question: What is the source of this world? He asked me to answer. His voice was calm and serious. I was so hungry for his seriousness after the moronic frivolity and despair of

hours in the mirror. I could not answer. Difficult, he said, reaching for his bell. I bowed and left.[29]

The scene of hanging from the branch by the teeth and the question about the source of the world are references to *koan*, the absurd riddles given by the Zen master to the novice to contemplate during meditation, estimating his progress on the road to enlightenment by his answers during their daily sessions. It seems then that Roshi may be symbolized by either the king or the ape (and see also poem 21).

**"What highway?"**—This word was not mentioned earlier, before the ape's question, but it is one of the key words in Cohen's work. For example, in the novel *The Favourite Game*, several pages are dedicated to the ceaseless driving of the protagonist Breavman and his friend Krantz on Canada's highways (mainly by night).[30] The highway suggests the voyage and the quest, but also the escape route for the man worried by commitment. "The Stranger Song" on Cohen's first album includes the lines: "And while he talks his dreams to sleep / you notice there's a highway / that is curling up like smoke above his shoulder."

## 3

This poem, which is one of the shortest in the book (along with poems 9 and 50, which are of similar length), describes poetically a process of study and a quest that run into many obstacles and difficulties. It evokes feelings of loneliness and guilt, a struggle between a person and his soul, failing to connect. The notion that something has been broken and cannot be mended still persists.

The poem reflects a well-known passage from *Sefer Ha-Zohar* or *The Book of Splendor* (in the common edition, Volume II, 99a) regarding the Torah, which is depicted in a fable as the beautiful beloved female secluded in a palace, who only reveals herself to her true lover stage by stage. Following is a partial translation:

29. Cohen, *Death of a Lady's Man*, 193; *Stranger Music*, 286.
30. Cohen, *The Favourite Game*, 91–95.

# I

> So it is with the Torah, which discloses her innermost secrets only to them who love her. She knows that whosoever is wise in heart hovers near the gates of her dwelling place day after day. What does she do? From her palace, she shows her face to him, and gives him a signal of love, and forthwith retreats back to her hiding place. Only he alone catches her message, and he is drawn to her with his whole heart and soul, and with all of his being. In this manner the Torah, for a moment, discloses herself in love to her lovers, so as to rouse them to renewed love . . . And when he arrives, she commences to speak with him, at first from behind the veil which she has hung before the words . . . Then she speaks to him behind a filmy veil of finer mesh, she speaks to him in riddles and allegories . . . When, finally, he is on near terms with her, she stands disclosed face to face with him, and holds converse with him concerning all of her secret mysteries, and all the secret ways which have been hidden in her heart from immemorial time.[31]

Cohen adapted the story for his own needs, as he did with the Zen story, even replacing the Torah with the soul, but the reference to the study of the Torah reemerges in the final sentence: **"This is what it's like to study without a friend."** This dictum is also taken from a well-known quote from the Mishnah: "Assume for yourself a master, acquire for yourself a friend" (m. Avot 1:6). Both a master and a companion are required for the process of study. According to the Babylonian Talmud: "Either friendship or death" (b. Taanit 23a). Even the greatest sages need a companion in order to maintain the dialogical process of study; the Talmudic sage Rabbi Johanan, after losing his companion Reish Lakish, also lost the sense of study and soon after lost his mind and died (b. Bava Metzia 84a).

In the Buddhist context there is the *Sangha*, the community or monastic order, which is the third of the "Three Jewels," following the *Buddha* (the enlightened one) and the *Dharma* (the

---

31. Scholem, *Zohar, the Book of Splendor*, 89–90.

teachings). Being part of a monastic community allows the novice to see his own reflection in the others and gain their support.

The above-quoted passage from *Sefer ha-Zohar* is also reflected in the prose passage "You Are Right, Sahara" in *Book of Longing*,[32] which combines Jewish, Christian and Buddhist imagery.

"**. . . a veil . . . a curtain**"—The speaker first mentions a veil, but during his attempt to mend things, this image changes to a curtain. Beside the element of hiding that is found in the episode from *Sefer ha-Zohar*, "curtain" has a special meaning in Jewish esoteric literature since its early stages, in the image of human souls woven into the curtain that hides the "Throne of Glory" (*kise hakavod*), which might be another source of the throne image in the previous poems. The curtain is also mentioned in poems 14 and 34, and it seems that Cohen was aware of the esoteric meaning of this image.

"**. . . a leaf**"—This image also appears in Cohen's songs, for example in "Sisters of Mercy": "If your life is a leaf that the seasons tear off and condemn / they will bind you with love that is graceful and green as a stem" (see also poem 29).

# 4

This poem describes a circular course of distancing oneself from the goal of the quest and returning to it in the end, following a failed attempt at self-advancement. It contains an important notion about the two types of will, as discussed below.

"**It was here that I found my will**"—The word "will," which appears here for the first time, is of great significance, and is repeated several times along the book (see poems 14, 35, 37, 40, 43, 45, 48). In a 1986 interview Cohen said regarding the question of the will:

> Well, we sense that there is a will that is behind all things, and we're also aware of our own will, and it's the distance between those two wills that creates the mystery that we call religion. It is the attempt to reconcile our will with another will that we can't quite put our finger on, but we feel is powerful and existent. It's the space between those two

---

32. Cohen, *Book of Longing*, 44.

# I

wills that creates our predicament... Somehow, in some way, we have to be a reflection of the will that is behind the whole mess. When you describe the outer husk of that will which is yours, which is your own tiny will—in all things mostly to succeed, to dominate, to influence, to be the king—when that will under certain conditions destroys itself, we come into contact with another will which seems to be much more authentic. But to reach that authentic will, our little will has to undergo a lot of battering. And it's not appropriate that our little will should be destroyed too often because we need it to interact with all the other little wills. From time to time things arrange themselves in such a way that that tiny will is annihilated, and then you're thrown back into a kind of silence until you can make contact with another authentic thrust of your being. And we call that prayer when we can affirm it. It happens rarely, but it happens in *Book of Mercy*, and that's why I feel it's kind of to one side, because I don't have any ambitions towards leading a religious life or a saintly life or a life of prayer. It's not my nature. I'm out on the street hustling with all the other wills. But from time to time you're thrown back to the point where you can't locate your tiny will, where it isn't functioning, and then you're invited to find another source of energy.[33]

    Cohen spoke of two types of will: an external one, which is powerful and "authentic," and an inner, "tiny" and private one. The inner will could be another expression of the "evil inclination" (see in the notes for poem 2), which is, according to Cohen and the traditional Jewish concept, necessary for our existence, but which is our duty to restrain. Cohen does not engage here with the question of the free will, but it seems to be lying in the background and is referred to more clearly later on (see poems 6 and 29). In most branches of the Jewish tradition (with the outstanding exception of the compilers of the sectarian writings found among the Dead Sea Scrolls who believed in predestination), determinism is opposed, and there is a duty to act, mend and fulfill the human potential. A person may choose between right and wrong, and is expected to

---

33. Sward, "An interview with Leonard Cohen," 166.

choose right ("choose life," Deut 30:19), although they may often fail, as the speaker here claims he did. According to the Kabbalah, human beings are the only creatures who possess a free will, and therefore have a crucial part to play in reuniting the higher and lower spheres of being and restoring the right order in the universe through prayer and fulfilment of the commandments. It should also be pointed out that "will" (Hebrew *ratzon*) is one of the attributes of *Keter*, the first *sefira* (see poem 5); the question of the will in the processes of emanation and creation is a very complex one, and the Kabbalists grappled with it at length.

**"With the two shields of bitterness and hope"**—As mentioned before, "The Shield" was one of the titles considered by Cohen for his book, and is repeated several times in it (see poems 8, 9, 20, 37, 42, 47). Bitterness serves as a shield against disappointment and due to past failures, but the hope that this time things may turn out right also serves as one. In the song "Lover, Lover, Lover," the first version of which Cohen wrote while volunteering to sing for Israeli soldiers in the Sinai Dessert during the October 1973 war, he sings: "And may the spirit of this song, / may it rise up pure and free. / May it be a shield for you, / a shield against the enemy."

**". . . to rescue the angel of song from the place where she had chained herself to her nakedness"**—This image is reminiscent of the picture on the back of Cohen's first album, *Songs of Leonard Cohen*, in which a naked female figure is depicted bound in chains and surrounded by flames of fire. According to Cohen, he found the picture in a New York store selling Mexican items, and the figure in it is an expression of the *anima sola*, the lonesome soul suffering in Purgatory before it can reach Heaven. In an early interview Cohen said that the picture depicts "the triumph of spirit over matter,"[34] but later explained that it conveys an ambiguous message of suffering and the release from it.

**". . . words"**—This word appears in both the first and last sentences of this poem. It refers to the speaker's creative struggle and his difficulty in finding the right expression. The words he is able to find express only the "tiny will" rather than the "authentic" one,

---

34. Burger, *Leonard Cohen on Leonard Cohen*, 21.

# I

and he is searching for words that will bring one will closer to the other. It is possible that the **"angel of song"** personifies the true observation, and the dialectical relation between observation and expression; she **"had chained herself to her nakedness,"** but her rescue from that place, and being covered with the private will, can lead to the true expression.

**"Adam"**—Together with the mention of **"ferns and women and snakes"** and the covering of nakedness, this may allude to the biblical story of the Garden of Eden in Gen 2–3 (see also poem 8). The **"angel of song"** here is the female partner of the primordial man, perhaps even Lilith, Adam's original partner according to the legend, and she sets Adam **"mysteriously free"** in a way that combines creativeness (song), eroticism, and faith (see further under poem 37). The speaker also expresses his wish for finding the correct words that relate to the "authentic" will, rather than his own tiny one, so the covering of the angel of song may symbolize the wish for purer, non-carnal expression. Incidentally, "Adam" is also the name of Cohen's son, who is mentioned (unnamed) in some of the following poems.

The idea of the "will" is also central to the final song on the *VP* album, "If It Be Your Will," arguably one of Cohen's most remarkable prayers. It refers to what Cohen called in the above-quoted interview the "authentic" will, not the human one. The common wording of Jewish prayers in English translation is "may it be your will," but here "may" is replaced by "if," which makes the expected response more doubtful or conditional. The song is quoted below verse by verse with some notes:

> If it be your will
> that I speak no more,
> and my voice be still
> as it was before;
> I will speak no more,
> I shall abide until
> I am spoken for,
> if it be your will.

The song opens with the willingness to be silent; the speaker's first act is listening as in the opening of the first poem of the book under discussion.

> If it be you will
> that a voice be true,
> from this broken hill
> I will sing to you.
> From this broken hill
> all your praises they shall ring
> if it be your will
> to let me sing.

The "broken hill" may allude to Jesus (in Matt 27:50–53 it is told that with Jesus' death the earth shook and the tombs broke open). The image may have occurred to Cohen also through the rocky view of Mount Baldy, where he would go to practice Zen.[35] Cohen rarely spoke about this song, but when introducing it during a concert in Linz on March 8, 1985, he said: "This is an old prayer it came to me to rewrite. It's about surrendering." A possible candidate for the old prayer alluded to by Cohen is the one uttered by Jesus at Gethsemane on the night of his arrest. According to Luke 22:42, he said: "Father, if you are willing, take this cup away from me. Yet not my will but yours be done." This can also explain the use of "if" in this song rather than "may," and the important presence of "the will" in both book and song. It should also be pointed out again that the motif of brokenness is central to this book in both its human and Kabbalistic meanings, as it is to other songs on the *VP* album such as "Hallelujah": "There's a blaze of light / in every word / it doesn't matter which you heard / the holy or the broken Hallelujah." In the above verse the speaker is asking for permission to sing from within his broken state (see further in the notes for poem 10).

> If it be your will
> If there is a choice
> Let the rivers fill
> Let the hills rejoice

---

35. Simmons, *I'm your Man*, 377.

# I

> Let your mercy spill
> On all these burning hearts in hell
> If it be your will
> To make us well

Here the speaker wishes to find a way out of the torturous silence while alluding to biblical verses, for example: "Let the rivers fill" alludes to verses such as Isa 41:18: "I will open rivers in high places, and fountains in the midst of the valleys: I will make the wilderness a pool of water, and the dry land springs of water," while "Let the hills rejoice" alludes to Ps 65:13: "and the hills are girded with joy," and also Amos 9:13: "the mountains shall drop sweet wine, and all the hills shall melt." Biblical verses always seem to be at the back of Cohen's mind, and to find expression in his writing.

> And draw us near
> And bind us tight
> All your children here
> In their rags of light
> In our rags of light
> All dressed to kill
> And end this night
> If it be your will
> If it be your will.

"Bind" goes back to the binding of Isaac in the Gen 22, about which Cohen recorded "The Story of Isaac" on his second album. Binding is also a frequent theme in the current book, and the speaker often asks to be bound (see poems 35, 41, and 48).

The expression "rags of light" stands out in this verse. Cohen must have been aware of the Midrash (in Bereshit Rabba 20:12) interpreting the verse in Gen 3:21: "And the Lord God made for Adam and for his wife garments of skin, and clothed them." The words "garments of skin" in Hebrew are: *kutnot 'or*; the 'o is the transliteration of the Hebrew letter 'Ayin, a guttural consonant which does not exist in European languages. The rabbis say that in one certain Torah scroll they found a different spelling: *kutnot 'or*, with the Hebrew letter Aleph, or A, which means "garments of light." This Midrash was further developed centuries later in the Kabbalah, as in this passage from *Sefer ha-Zohar* (I, 36b): "To begin with these were garments of light, now that they have sinned—garments of skin," which means that before the Fall, the human body was spiritual in nature and wrapped in light, but having sinned became corporal and needed a cover of skin. Cohen took the Midrash a step further too, replacing "garments" with "rags," and adding the poignant expression "dressed to kill" with its various implications. *Book of Mercy* echoes the song in several places, with lines such as: **"Blessed are you who dressed the shivering spirit in skin"** (14), and **"We stand in rags"** (15). One more echo of the song occurs in poem 35: **"If it be your will, accept the longing truth beneath this wild activity."**

The final image in the song is the long night, for the end of which the speaker is yearning. As often with Cohen, this image combines the actual, in this case the night, with the symbolized, which here refers to the soul's suffering and yearning alluding to the "Dark Night of the Soul," the long poem by St. John of the Cross (San Juan de la Cruz in his native Spanish). The "dark night" symbolizes the continuous struggle of the soul on its path seeking the absolute, an experience familiar to Cohen.

## 5

The poem opens with a cry for rest which is not heeded and ends with a prayer to gain the Sabbath peace. In between a reconnection with tradition takes place, first impatiently, but then more favorably through the response of the personified Torah. The speaker then goes through three stages: first he desires rest as a remedy against panic and fruitless idleness, then he reconnects with the Torah, still reluctantly, but once realizing its value, he gains the crown. Further progress occurs in the following poem.

**"Pharaoh"**—Symbolizes the forces of evil and impurity, the "other side" (*Sitra Achara*) according to the Kabbalah.

**"You have sealed every gate but this one"**—The gates are the gates of heaven, a metaphor first appearing in Gen 28:18, following Jacob's dream. In Hebrew, "heaven's gate" is *Sha'ar ha-Shamayim*,

# I

which is also the name of Cohen's family's synagogue in Montreal. It is a common Jewish perception that once the temple in Jerusalem was destroyed in 70 CE, heavens' gates were sealed, but various sources give exceptions to the rule. According to one version (Midrash Tehilim 4:3): "Gates of prayer are sometimes open and sometime locked, but gates of mercy are never locked." Another version is in the Talmud (b. Berachot 32b): "Rabbi Elazar said: Since the day the Temple was destroyed the gates of prayer were locked . . . Yet . . . the gates of tears were not locked." The expression "gates of mercy" does not appear in the book, but many years later it was included in the song "Come Healing" on the album *Old Ideas* (2012), which is also one of Cohen's distinct prayer songs, containing a large assortment of *Book of Mercy* key words, including "the Name," "brokenness," "light," "darkness," "solitude," "longing," and "heart."

"**'I do not put my trust in man, nor do I place reliance on an angel'**"—Biblical verses behind this declaration could include Ps 146:3: "Don't put your trust in human leaders; no human being can save you," and Job 4:18: "God does not trust his heavenly servants; he finds fault even with his angels." From the opposite direction there is Ps 40:5: "Happy is the man that had made the Lord his trust."

"**Immediately the Torah sang to him**"—The Torah is personified here again, as in the *Zohar* paragraph quoted in the notes for poem 3. The contact with the Torah takes the speaker back to his earliest childhood memories.

"**. . . the weightless crown . . . The crown that leaps up from the letters**"—The crown is a symbol with numerous meanings which appears here for the first time but will reappear in several other poems (6, 10, 36, 48). It can refer to the actual crown of the king who was mentioned before and will be mentioned again. There are "crowns" over some of the letters in the Torah scroll alluded to here and there is also a crown for the Torah scroll itself, which is a well-known article of traditional Jewish decorative art usually made of silver. There are also the crowns of the righteous mentioned below and the crown of thorns placed on Jesus' head.

Of great importance is the Kabbalistic meaning. "Crown" (*Keter*) is the name of the first of the ten *sefirot* which mediates between the rest of them and the Infinite (*Ein Sof*), the unknowable source of emanation (and according to some Kabbalists, is also unknowable) and is the source of the flow of vitality going through the *sefirot* and into the worlds which is described here in the poetical image of the **"dew that gives the grass to drink beads out of the darkness."** The father and mother mentioned later on may also have a Kabbalistic meaning: "Wisdom" (*Chochmah*) and "Understanding" (*Binah*), the *sefirot* that receive the flow from *Keter* and pass it on to the lower seven are known also as "the higher father and mother." The *sefirot* emanate from one to the next—"like lighting a candle with a candle" is the common image—and not through creation, unlike the material world which was created at a later stage. "Crowns" is also an alternative name for the *sefirot*. The speaker says that the crown **"raises up no man a king above his company"** perhaps because the Torah is available to all who seek it.

**"Lead me deep into your Sabbath"**—The Sabbath here, besides the day of rest, can also be a symbol of the ultimate redemption of the world, the eternal Sabbath. The Sabbath is also one of the attributes of *Malchut*-"Kingdom," the tenth *sefirah* which is associated also with King David.

**". . . let me sit beneath the mighty ones whom you have crowned forever"**—The background to this image might be the Talmudic passage concerning the messianic future or the existence of souls in Heaven: "The World-to-Come is not like this world. In the World-to-Come there is no eating, no drinking, no procreation, no business negotiations, no jealousy, no hatred, and no competition. Rather, the righteous sit with their crowns upon their heads, enjoying the splendor of the Divine Presence" (b. Berachot, 17a). Also in the *Zohar*, in a passage about the righteous who weaved their good deeds into garments for their souls to wear in the World-to-Come, it is said in part: "all they who by righteousness have gained for themselves a garment of glory made of their days are in the future world crowned like patriarchs, with crowns

I

from the stream that flows unceasing into the Garden of Eden" (I, 224b).[36] "Garden of Eden" is one of the many attributes of the tenth *sefirah, Malchut*.

"**. . . mother . . . war . . . father**"—The song "Night Comes On" on the *VP* album has a certain parallel: the first verse is about the mother and the second begins with fighting in a war and then mentioning the father (see also notes for poem 9).


## 6

From the failures and loneliness of adulthood, the speaker wishes to return to the security of childhood and the community. The spiral-like process of rejoining, as depicted in the first five poems, reaches its peak here although soon afterwards the inevitable sliding down will occur.

"**Sit down, master, on this rude chair of praises**"—The master here may be Roshi, but it can also refer to the divinity. The "Throne of Glory" (see poems 1 and 3) is depicted here as having been created by the speaker's prayers and it is "rude" because his words are inadequate. Still, it is a step forward from the **"throne of unemployment"** in the previous poem.

"**. . . great decrees of freedom**"—This dialectical expression may again have to do with either the guidence of Roshi or the teaching of the Torah and is also related to the issue of free will (see poem 4).

"**. . . to do my daily task**"—Contrary to the Sabbath rest yearned for in poem 5, here the speaker gets down to work. Apart from his daily task (writing and composing), this can also hint at the daily cultic work of the priests at the Jerusalem temple. Cohen was fascinated by the fact that his family name made him, according to the Jewish tradition, a scion of the priestly tribe and referred to it often in his work and interviews; see, for example, the *Book of Longing* passage "Moving Into A Period," which is rich in biblical

---

36. Scholem, *Zohar, the Book of Splendor*, 67–68.

and Kabbalistic allusions (such as the Bride and Bridegroom, see also in poem 29):

> But there will be a Cross, a sign, that some will understand; a secret meeting, a warning, a Jerusalem hidden in Jerusalem. I will be wearing white clothes, as usual, and I will enter the Innermost Place as I have done generation upon generation, to entreat, to plead, to justify. I will enter the chamber of the Bride and Bridegroom, and no one will follow me.[37]

The core imagery in the above passage is taken from the description of the cultic rituals performed by the High Priest (*kohen gadol*) during *Yom Kippur*, the Day of Atonement, the only day in the year when the High Priest entered the Holy of Holies, the innermost chamber of the Jerusalem Temple, as described in the tractate Yoma of the Mishnah. The greater part of the tractate is recited in the synagogue during the afternoon prayers on the Day of Atonement (*Seder ha-ʿAvodah*).

**"Out of mist and dust you have fashioned me to know the numberless worlds between the crown and the kingdom"**— When the dust-made body gains a spirit (Gen 2:7), human beings become creatures capable of grasping the divine. "Crown" is the first *sefirah* and "Kingdom" is the tenth and last one. However, the principal structure of the ten *sefirot* is only the beginning, since the *sefirot* reflect each other creating dynamics that greatly increase the numerical possibilities as elaborated in the Kabbalistic literature.

In the song "It's Torn" on the posthumously-released album *Thanks for the Dance*, Cohen has the line: "It's torn in the highest from kingdom to crown," the opposite direction than in the above quote (probably for the sake of the rhyme). That song has numerous other lines and expressions connecting it with *Book of Mercy* such as: "It's torn where there's beauty, it's torn where there's death / It's torn where there's mercy but torn somewhat less," and "The name has no number, not even the one." It is one more formidable example of the way in which Cohen combined various meanings

---

37. Cohen, *Book of Longing*, 34.

# I

into one song: the erotic stands out, but all along it contains expressions that hint at a second layer, that of the speaker's relations with the divine. And like *Book of Mercy*, it deals with the efforts to mend a state of brokenness which are only partially or temporarily successful.

**"Let nine men come to lift me into their prayer"**—Ten is the minimal quorum (*minyan*) required in traditional Jewish practice for praying and reading the Torah in public. In tradition-bound communities, like the one Cohen grew up in, only men were counted. Reform, and later Conservative, communities in North America and elsewhere now also include women in the quorum.

**"Blessed be the name of the glory of the kingdom forever and forever"**—This is the verse recited in the daily prayers after the first verse of the *Shema*. However, Cohen gives it a little twist, writing "the kingdom" instead of "His kingdom," and see poem 48 where this verse is quoted once again with a different twist.

## 7

Following the gradual progress toward the renewal of connection with the tradition and the community—the Jewish one, although possibly also the Zen-practicing one—as depicted in the previous poems, in this one the speaker encounters a setback and the renewal of the feeling of being exiled and even defiled. The speaker also exhibits compulsive behavior with recurring circles of pleasure and guilt.

**"I pushed my body from one city to another, one rooftop to another, to see a woman bathing"**—The speaker identifies here with King David, both as a sinner who repented his crime (and whose sin was, among other things, sexual), and as the composer of the Psalms in which he expressed his pain and regret. David admitted his sin of seducing Bathsheba—whom he saw naked from his rooftop—and having her husband Uriah killed, immediately on hearing the prophet Nathan's allegation, saying: "I have sinned against the Lord" (2 Sam 12:13). Ps 51 is associated with the same affair and in verse 6 David says: "Against Thee, Thee only, have I sinned, and done that which is evil in Thy sight." In the current poem the punishment and misery that follow begin in the throat, therefore associated with singing. All these motifs come together in the song "Hallelujah" on the *VP* album. The song opens with David playing music, followed by his seeing a woman bathing on the roof and then turning to the pain of love (it should be noted in passing that the "you" addressed in the song changes identity and may be the divine, a lover, David, and perhaps the speaker himself; this is one of Cohen's familiar poetic devices). In later verses the song speaks about faith, of knowing the Name and of the creative impulse, ending with the lines: "And even though / it all went wrong / I'll stand before the Lord of Song / with nothing on my lips but Hallelujah." In subsequent live performances of the song Cohen replaced the first three verses with different ones, but left the fourth, just quoted, as the final one. The story of David and Bathsheba always held an important place for Cohen, as in the early poem "Before the Story," which is dedicated to David's life-story and includes the verse:

> Far from the roof,
> the king, David,
> begins the ageless psalm
> which rings through caves
> and tears the cobwebs
> from the sleeper's face[38]

**"Then the exile closed around me"**—The exile here is of both body and soul, using the powerful image of Jewish reality being exiled from their land and having to dwell among other nations (see further in the notes for poem 24).

**"Then the Law shining"**—When capitalized, "the Law" is usually a synonym for the Torah, which is mentioned literally in the book only three times ("law" is mentioned ten times; and see poem 29). At this stage the Torah is still remote and too clean for the speaker, who feels polluted. Another relevant song on the *VP* album is "The Law," with its refrain: "There's a Law, there's an Arm,

---

38. Cohen, *The Spice-Box of Earth*, 16–17.

# I

there's a Hand." Like other songs on the album, it can be read in two ways: as speaking to a woman and talking about their relationship, or as speaking to a higher entity, as common in the book. Cohen says, for example: "I'm not asking for mercy / Not from the man / You just don't ask for mercy / While you're still on the stand." The implication here may be that he will not ask a human being for mercy, but he may ask a different entity for it. Introducing the song in Warsaw (1985) Cohen said: "Beyond the sovereignty of any nation there is a judgment, there is a reward, there is a punishment, there is a law, there is an arm, there is a hand."

**"How long . . ."**—This expression, repeated here twice, must derive from the intreating language of the Psalms, for example: "How long, O Lord, will you forget me for ever? How long will you hide your face from me? How long shall I take counsel in my soul, having sorrow in my heart by day? How long shall my enemy be exalted over me?" (Ps 13:2–3).

**"O master of my breath"**—This can refer also to Zen meditation in which special attention is paid to correct breathing. The breathing motif is repeated several times along the book (see poems 23, 28, 30, 47, and 48 among others). Earlier Cohen was quoted on the similarity he found between the Kabbalistic ideas and Zen teaching regarding in and out breath.

**". . . gather my heart toward the gravity of your name"**—"Gravity" has a double meaning here. See also the later poem of the same title.[39]

**"Form me again with an utterance"**—The creation by utterance is one of the basic principles in both Judaism and Christianity (see further in the notes for poem 14 below). The speaker wishes to be recreated, free of defilement.

**". . . and open my mouth with your praise"**—According to Ps 51:17, and the first verse of the 'Amidah prayer recited thrice daily: "My Lord, open my lips and my mouth shall declare your praise."

---

39. Cohen, *Book of Longing*, 212.

## 8

As in the previous poem, here too there is a feeling of distress expressed through the constant falling, but by the end of the poem the fall finds direction and hope is rekindled. The fall itself is also celebrated as a thing of beauty.

"... falls ... falling"—The word "fall" has a stronger connotation in English than in Hebrew concerning the story of the Garden of Eden and the expulsion of human beings from it. This is due to the Christian layer added on to the Jewish story, that of the "original sin," due to which the whole of humanity was defiled and can only be saved by Jesus Christ's grace and his spilled blood. The fall is the human condition (*conditio humana*), or the **"human accident"** in this poem. There is no escaping it, but solace may still be found.

"... he falls radiantly"—This image brings to mind Lucifer, the fallen angel. Lucifer means "light bearer" in Latin, and refers to Venus when it appears as the morning star (according to the Vulgate translation of Is 14:12). In Christianity Lucifer is known as the angel who rebelled against God and fell from Heaven. The speaker here seems to embrace this figure. He too is a sinner and he too is falling, but it is a beautiful fall, like a meteor. He falls but does not crash because there is someone who holds him in his falling and helps him find his place. In the song from the *VP* album mentioned above, "The Law," the speaker says: "I fell with my angel / Down the chain of command," which is another possible allusion to Lucifer.

**"Blessed are you, clasp of falling"**—This expression derives again from the *'Amidah* prayer, in turn based on Ps 145:14: "The Lord upholds all that fall." It should be noted that the speaker (or the figure he identifies with) is falling towards the light, taking on its radiance, but is not absorbed by it; as said earlier, Cohen drew a line at the mystical experience he was supposed to have wished for and he always remained connected with mundane reality, committed to the here and now (see also the notes for poem 39).

I

**"Blessed are you, shield of falling"**—Another occurrence of "shield" (see poem 4). Also in the *Amidah* prayer: "O king, [you are] a helper, a savior and a shield. Blessed are you, Lord, shield of Abraham" (and see poem 20).

**". . . he finds his place . . . he enters into the place of his fall"**—"Place" is another one of those words repeated often in the book (30 times, in one half of the poems). In Hebrew, *ha-Makom* ("the place") is one of God's attributes, and this may be the intention here too (see also poem 29: **"your eternal place,"** and also 33, 44, 47, and 50). In some other cases, the word indicates the place painful for the speaker. The later song "Show Me The Place," on the album *Old Ideas*, echoes *Book of Mercy* in the position of the speaker and in several expressions (see also under poem 45).

**"Blessed are you, embrace of the falling"**—This is the third blessing in this poem directed towards the divine in a gradual process that goes from hard ("clasp," "shield") to tender ("embrace").

**". . . foundation of the light"**—"Foundation" is the name of the ninth *sefirah* (*Yesod*), and the expression here may allude to it. When the *sefirot* are depicted in the form of a man, *Yesod* is regarded as the male organ. "Foundation" is mentioned in the book five times (once in the plural form), and always in the possessive form with another noun: "light" (8, 46), "your holiness" (10), "unity" (29), "the night" (42).

## 9

This is one of the shortest poems in the book (similar in length to poems 3 and 50), but the three key words—"shield," "name" and "mercy"—all appear in it: "shield" at the beginning, "mercy" at the end, and "name" in the middle, three times. "Name" is repeated in the book about 60 times, occurring in about half of its poems (for "mercy" see under poem 1, and for "shield" under poem 4). Still, the outstanding word in this poem is "loneliness," another important word in the book. It also appears in poems 6, 11, 13, 16, and 35, while "solitude" appears in poems 15, 34, 36, 39, 47, and 48.

"**Blessed are you who has given each man a shield of loneliness**"—"Loneliness" and the adjective "lonely" often appear in Cohen's songs. For example, as in the current poem, "loneliness" and "sin" appear in proximity in "Sisters of Mercy": "When you're not feeling holy, your loneliness says that you've sinned." In the current poem loneliness serves as a shield, as bitterness did before (see poem 4). In the song "Suzanne" Cohen referred through an unusual image to Jesus' loneliness on the cross, calling it "his lonely wooden tower" (changing, in some live performances, "lonely" to "lonesome," a word which appears in some other of his songs, such as "A Bunch of Lonesome Heroes" on the album *Songs from a Room*).

"**. . . your name, which is beyond all consolations that are uttered on this earth**"—This is a variation on a verse from the *Kaddish*: "May his great name be blessed . . . beyond all the blessings and hymns, praises and consolations that are uttered in this world." The *Kaddish* is a hymn in praise of God which is included in all daily prayers when recited in public, but it is also associated with bereavement because people in mourning recite the "Mourner's *Kaddish*." This must have been the association for Cohen too and therefore this allusion appears in a poem in which loneliness is the main theme. Cohen's father died when he was nine—the number of the current poem—and he seems to have never overcome his loss. His mother died in 1978, a few years before the writing of *Book of Mercy*. Cohen expressed his orphanhood in the song "Night Comes On" on the *VP* album. The song contains five verses, each of which has associations with the current book. In the first verse the speaker visits his mother's grave, tells her of his fears and she promises to stay at his side, sending him back into the world. In the second verse he speaks with his father against the background of war experiences (the father served as an officer in WWI, the son encountered war in the Sinai desert in 1973). The third verse depicts a crisis with his female companion and mentions his children who ask him to play (see the following poem, and also poems 25 and 33). The fourth verse mentions prayer and the yearning for protective love extended by a muse-like female

I

figure who comes and departs but leaves him with a song. The fifth verse includes several images repeated in the *Book of Mercy* such as crickets, a cat, and a bar for meeting friends. The song ends with the mother's rejection of her son's death wish and her sending him back to face the world.

**10**

This is the first thanksgiving hymn in the book, although poem 8 may be partially so. Difficulties and obstacles are again encountered, but they are depicted as positive experiences. The speaker's family too appears here for the first time and the poem ends with his words of love for his children.

 "**You have sweetened your word on my lips**"—Several biblical verses might be behind this line, for example Ps 119:103: "How sweet are your words to my taste, sweeter than honey to my mouth."

 "**From Abraham to Augustine**"—Including both Judaism and Christianity (Abraham is mentioned also in poems 11, 14, and 20).

 "**. . . the nations have not known you**"—Cohen dedicates poem 27 to the historical and political issue that is only hinted at here.

 "**You bound me . . . as you bind every man, except the ones who need no binding**"—The story of the binding of Isaac in Gen 22 is of special importance for Cohen who used it for expressing both personal affliction and political protest in his song "Story Of Isaac" on his second album, *Songs from a Room*. His personal binding to the story is revealed in this song by the line: "I was nine years old," his age when his father died. The verb "to bind" appears in the book in various declinations fifteen times, often expressing the wish to be bound (for example poems 35, 42, and 48. For another allusion to the biblical binding story see poem 22, and for another possible interpretation of the verb, the notes for poem 48).

 "**. . . my fingerprints**"—Cohen has a song titled "Fingerprints" on the album *Death of a Ladies' Man* (1977).

**"You led me to this field where I dance with a broken knee"**—Cohen told Michael Benazon that sometime around 1976 he had an accident in which he tore the meniscus on his knee and for a while was unable to sit in Zen meditation and that he then "started studying Judaism in a more or less deliberate way" and that "*Book of Mercy* came out of that period."[40]

As indicated before (see poem 4), "broken" is a key word for Cohen, appearing in at least fifteen of his recorded songs. In the book, forms of "break" appear sixteen times of which "broken" appears ten times (poems 10, 12, 17, 27, 28, 38, 40, 46, and twice in poem 49). Being broken is a fundamental state of existence for Cohen although it is not a state in which he remains crushed but rather comes out of as in this case, dancing. Awareness of the broken state of the universe in the Kabbalistic and other senses leads to the effort of mending.

**". . . a crown of darkness and light"**—The crown is an image that reappears throughout the book (see poems 5 and 6 above, 36 and 48 below). The combination of darkness and light was probably inspired by a famous passage from the *Zohar* (I, 15a) which opens with the mention of "the will" and of "the king":

> "In the beginning" (Gen 1:1)—when the will of the King began to take effect, he engraved signs into the heavenly spheres. Within the most hidden recess a dark flame issued from the mystery of *eyn sof*, the Infinite, like a fog forming in the unformed—enclosed in the ring of that sphere, neither white nor black, neither red nor green, of no color whatever . . .[41]

Another possible source from the *Zohar* is in a long passage about the first light which says among other things (I, 32a):

> This light emerged from the darkness which was hewed out by the strokes of the Most Secret; and likewise, from the light which was hidden away, through some secret path, there was hewed out the darkness of the lower world

---

40. Benazon, "Leonard Cohen of Montreal," 53.
41. Scholem, *Zohar, the Book of Splendor*, 27.

I

in which inheres light. This light is called "night" in the verse, "and the darkness He called night" (Gen 1:5).[42]

Years later Cohen would open the song "Boogie Street" on the album *Ten New Songs* (2001) with the lines: "O Crown of light, O Darkened One / I never thought we'd meet." As is often seen in these notes, Cohen remained faithful to the images that inspired him deeply throughout his life. On "darkness" see more under poems 32, 45, and 46.

"**. . . and tears to greet my enemy**"—This line, together with the earlier one that mentions a broken knee, alludes to the story of Jacob in Gen 32–33: his struggle with a "man" that left him wounded in the leg (32:24–25, and see a clearer reference in poem 27) and enemies who greet each other with tears (33:4).

"**Who can tell of your glory, who can number your forms**"— A possible source is Ps 106:2: "Who can express the mighty acts of the Lord, or make all His praise to be heard?" However, beyond this and other biblical verses, another important source of influence on Cohen may have been the large-scale poem *Keter Malchut* ("Royal Crown") by the eleventh century Spanish-Jewish poet and philosopher Solomon Ibn Gabirol, one of the greatest Hebrew poets of all time, who belonged to what is known as the "Golden Age" of Hebrew poetry in Moslem Spain, or Al-Andalus. The poem is included in some of the prayer books for the High Holidays. This outstanding work is simultaneously a prayer, a philosophical poem praising God's greatness (while emphasizing the difficulties in using human language to do so), and a very personal expression of the poet's feelings. The poem is divided into forty sections and has many parallels to *Book of Mercy*. Sections 10 to 32 of *Keter Malchut* open with questions such as "who can know," "who can understand" and so on, regarding God and his actions, as in our current poem. Section 25 deals with the angels, sections 26 and 27 mention the Throne of Glory, and section 25 describes the pleasures of the souls in Heaven and their rest (see the end of poem 5). In sections 33 to 40 the speaker repents of his sins and thanks

---

42. Scholem, *Zohar, the Book of Splendor*, 30.

God for his grace, while in section 36 he says that since his evil inclination incited him, he is left with nothing but God's mercy, and he asks for it again in sections 39 and 40. The message of both *Keter Malchut* and *Book of Mercy* is similar: it is impossible to truly know God, but there is still a duty to praise his acts in the world. Sin is inescapable, but it is still possible to ask for mercy. Note also expressions such as "between the crown and the kingdom" in poem 6, which may have been inspired by the title of *Keter Malchut*, besides the titles of the *sefirot*. Because of this proximity in spirit and detail it is at least likely that Solomon ibn Gabirol's work was another model for Cohen's besides the Psalms, which were in any case a model for his predecessor as well.

## 11

This poem which opens and ends with the mention of a prayer, expresses a desire to get closer to the tradition although still not without difficulties. Simultaneously, and as is common with Cohen, the erotic aspect is also rekindled but collides with the fear of a permanent and binding relationship with a woman.

"... **the pages of Abraham ... one newly circumcised**"—This alludes to the covenant between God and man which circumcision symbolizes, but may also have erotic connotations (and women appear in the following line). According to Gen 17, Abraham was the first man to be circumcised and at a very advanced age which must have been extremely painful. It is a trauma that requires healing but the speaker, who has been reconnecting with his tradition—and therefore may consider himself **"newly circumcised"**—trusts this process. In the Bible circumcision also has the metaphorical usage of cleansing the heart, for example Deut 10:16: "Circumcise then the foreskin of your heart, and be no more stiffnecked."

**"Various families"**—These may be connected with the nations mentioned in the previous poem. The various chairs offered to the speaker may symbolize different traditions or groups. In the song "Last Year's Man" on his third album Cohen has the lines: "I came upon a wedding that old families had contrived; / Bethlehem the bridegroom, / Babylon the bride." This song also contains many expressions of the personal suffering, biblical imagery, and spiritual and erotic yearnings which are expressed throughout *Book of Mercy*. This may also allude to the creation of a family in the domestic sense of which Cohen by this time had more than one.

"... **the woman who carries me off**"—This woman is preferred to the ones who earlier offered him beauty and kindness. She seems to be the sexually alluring woman with whom he can have a risky, highly-charged short-term affair, rather than a stable relationship. But in a typical double meaning, the woman mentioned could also symbolize the spiritual quest: a hand-written "poem" beginning "Dear Roshi" in *Book of Longing* appears next to a drawing of a voluptuous woman in the familiar style of temple sculptures in India.[43] Cohen apologizes to Roshi for not being able to help him "because I met this woman," hinting perhaps to his flirt with Indian philosophy which drew him away from Zen practice (the poem "Leaving Mt. Baldy" is printed on the opposite page). In the current book we also find the feminine image of the personified Torah along with that of *Malchut* (Kingdom), the *sefirah* representing the feminine aspect; one of its symbols is the moon which is mentioned both at the beginning and end of this poem.

"**I will always sit with the family of loneliness**"—This surprising oxymoron draws our attention again to the important place ascribed by the speaker to loneliness and solitude (see poem 9). He may not idealize it, but at least in some cases he seems to prefer it. It may also refer to the Jewish people and their state of exile (see poem 7 above and 24 below). The image of the family appears also in poem 23, in which the speaker's "sister" could refer to Christianity.

"...**under the shadow of the tabernacle of peace**"—The "tabernacle of peace" is a post-biblical expression which appears in the *Siddur* especially in the *Arvit* or evening prayer, in which the community entreats: "Spread over us Your tabernacle of mercy and peace." The speaker here enters the mode of solitary prayer for long periods, detaching himself from his surroundings. Even

43. Cohen, *Book of Longing*, 23.

his cat has to await his return. The need to find a protective hiding place in the face of a collapsing reality is expressed in the song "Dance Me to the End of Love" on the *VP* album with the line: "Raise a tent of shelter now, though every thread is torn."

## 12

This poem expresses the painful contradiction between the beauty that can be found in this world and human suffering depicted in great detail, while imploring mercy and relating to the speaker's work ("bitter song").

"**. . . you whom David found in hell**"—Among the Psalms attributed to David, whose life after having committed his great sin deteriorated into a series of ongoing catastrophes, there is Ps 18:5–7: "The cords of Death compassed me, and the floods of Belial assailed me. The cords of Sheol surrounded me; the snares of Death confronted me. In my distress I called upon the Lord, and cried unto my God; out of His temple He heard my voice, and my cry came before Him unto His ears." "Sheol," which is here transliterated from the Hebrew, is sometimes substituted for "Hell" in translations, although they are not identical, and this is what Cohen must have had in mind in writing this verse (see also Ps 139:7–10). According to the Catholic faith, although this is not mentioned in the Scriptures, during the three days between his crucifixion and when he arose from the dead, Jesus descended into Hell (*Descensus Christi ad Inferos*, or "Harrowing of Hell"), and released the souls of the righteous who preceded him including David. This is one of the typical scenes depicted in Christian art and is mentioned also in the Apostles' Creed. This might also have had its impact on Cohen here.

"**The skeletons are waiting for your famous mechanical salvation**"—This must refer to Ezek 37:1–14, where the prophet sees the vision of the revival of dry bones. The word "mechanical" may also suggest *deus ex machina*, the divine intervention that can bring about a favorable outcome against all expectations. It could also be one of the references to the Holocaust found throughout

## I

Cohen's work. The song "Dance Me to the End of Love" on the *VP* album does not include such a clear reference, but Cohen said that the inspiration for it came from those who were made to play music at the death camps.[44] See also poem 19.

"... **radiant one, sourceless, source of light**"—The image here may relate to the Kabbalistic notion that *Ein Sof* itself is sourceless, but is the source of light radiating through the *sefirot*. It may also be a variation on the "unmoved mover" of Aristotelian philosophy, adopted in the medieval philosophy and theology of the three monotheistic religions, or the "causeless cause" in various thought systems.

"... **black Hebrew gibberish of pruned grapevines**"—This graphic metaphor could refer to the books written in Hebrew script which was still difficult for him to decipher. It may also allude to Leviticus 25, a chapter already mentioned above in the context of the Jubilee, and twice again below (poems 23 and 27) in other contexts. Lev 25:4–5 reads: "But in the seventh year shall be a sabbath of solemn rest for the land, a sabbath unto the Lord; thou shalt neither sow thy field, nor prune thy vineyard. That which groweth of itself of thy harvest thou shalt not reap, and the grapes of thy undressed vine thou shalt not gather; it shall be a year of solemn rest for the land." These verses speak of the seventh year, while the following verses (8–17) speak of the Jubilee, which as mentioned in the Introduction did not bring Cohen the deliverance he hoped for. Both "grapevine" and "vineyard" are rich in symbolism across the Bible and beyond.

"... **the impeccable landscape of fields and milky towns**"—This description must refer to southern France where parts of the book were written. In the irony-filled passage "Why I Love France," Cohen mentioned "the milky towns of the Luberon,"[45] the area of Provence where his erstwhile partner Suzanne and their children were then living (see also poem 38).

"... **and do not separate me from my tears**"—He might have been expected to ask for the opposite, but as often along the

---

44. Simmons, *I'm Your Man*, 318.
45. Cohen, *Book of Longing*, 115.

book the speaker does not expect to be disconnected with reality which necessarily contains pain as well as other feelings. He even asks for tears on several occasions (see, for example, poems 15 and 36; "tears" appear twelve times in the book).

## 13

It is probably not a coincidence that this poem is numbered 13 which is the age when a Jewish boy celebrates his Bar-Mitzvah, becoming an adult from the religious obligations point of view. The poem highlights the study of the Torah as **"a Jew's business."**

**"Friend"**—He is the one who was missing earlier, in poem 3. This could be either a generic term or a specific person from Cohen's life such as his maternal grandfather, Solomon Klonitzki-Kline, who was an illustrious rabbi and scholar, and whom he depicted in his long prose-poem "Lines from My Grandfather's Journal."[46] It could also be his oldest friend, the sculptor Mort Rosengarten (who is depicted as Krantz in Cohen's first novel, *The Favourite Game*) with whom he continued frequenting Jewish restaurants in Montreal, or the poet Irving Layton who was a mentor and a close friend of Cohen's and with whom he used to spend long hours reading and analyzing poetry. Layton's original name was Israel Lazarovitch, as mentioned in Cohen's poem "Last Dance at the Four Penny."[47]

**"If you provoke, I accept the challenge"**—This poem reflects the process of Talmudic study and argument.

**"... or we can take our places in the Sanhedrin"**—The Sanhedrin was the assembly of rabbis appointed to sit as a tribunal. It existed for several centuries before and after the Common Era.

**"... those great cubes of diamond that our teacher Moses shouldered down the mountain"**—A poetic image for the tablets of the Torah written by God and given to Moses in Sinai (Exod

---

46. Cohen, *The Spice-Box of Earth*, 77–83.
47. Cohen, *The Spice-Box of Earth*, 64–65.

# I

32:15–16). "Our teacher Moses" (*Moshe Rabenu*) is the traditional way of referring to the law-giver.

"**You want . . . I suggest . . .**"—The friends' argument is part of the study process. The first position expressed here may reflect a more earth-bound view, while the second one is more Kabbalistic in its approach alluding to the divine world.

"**. . . the sun by day, and the moon and stars by night, will shine through them**"—This wording follows biblical verses such as Ps 121:6: "The sun shall not smite you by day, Nor the moon by night," and Ps 136:8–9: "The sun to rule by day . . . The moon and stars to rule by night."

"**. . . which would include the light of the celestial bodies within the supernal radiance of the cubes**"—This image may allude to the divine light flowing through the *sefirot* and expressed through the Torah (see also "radiant one" in the previous poem). The "celestial bodies" are also symbols used for the *sefirot*: "sun" for *Tif'ert* (Beauty / Mercy) and "moon" for *Malchut* (Kingdom / Presence).

"**The dust mingles with the mist, our nostrils widen**"—This may allude to Gen 2:7: "Then the LORD God formed man of the dust of the ground, and breathed into his nostrils the breath of life; and man became a living soul" (see also poem 6 above, and 28 below). The joint study of the Torah and the dialogue between them raises the friends up to their full human and Jewish potential.

"**. . . now we can get down to a Jew's business**"—This can sound ironic because a common unfavorable image of the Jews is that their business is to make money, but here it is shown to be the serious study of the Torah. In the song "The Future" on the album of the same title (1992), Cohen declares: "I'm the little jew [sic] / who wrote the Bible" (and see the interview with Kurtzweil with a similar heading). After several missteps, the speaker finally overcame the obstacles that prevented him from engaging with the dedicated study of the Torah.

## 14

This poem can be read as a thanksgiving hymn for deliverance, while dealing with several major issues that come up throughout the book as specified below. It is the only poem to which Cohen added an explanatory footnote.

"**Who put a curtain over a house**"—The curtain is a recurring element (see poems 3, 12, and 34) and so are several other ways of covering and hiding, which stand out in this poem.

"**Blessed be Ishmael, who taught us how to cover ourselves**"—The story of Ishmael (his name means "God will hear") is mainly in Genesis chapters 16, 17, and 21, and as explained in Cohen's footnote he "is traditionally considered the father of the Arab nation." The biblical story does not mention covering, but Cohen may have associated it with an Arab custom. It is also possible that he was familiar with a certain Talmudic passage containing an argument on whether the prayer shawl should be laid only on the body or also cover the head and part of the face, "in the manner of the wrapping of the Ishmaelites" (b. Moed Katan 24a).

"**Blessed are you who dressed the shivering spirit in a skin**"—See the explanation of "garments of skin" in the notes for poem 4.

"**Who made a fence of changing stars around your wisdom . . . sheltered understanding**"—"Wisdom" (*Chochma*) and "Understanding" (*Binah*) are the second and the third *sefirot* known also as the "higher father and mother" (see also notes for poem 5). For "a fence" see poem 21.

"**Blessed be the teacher of my heart, on his throne of patience**"—This may refer to Roshi (see poems 1, 2, and 21). The line "Are you the teachers of my heart?" appears in the song "Teachers" on Cohen's first album. As in previous occurrences of the throne in the book, this could also allude to God who in the prayers for the High Holidays is beseeched to "Rise from your throne of judgment and sit on your throne of mercy" (see notes for poem 1).

"**Blessed are you who circled desire with a blade**"—This could be an allusion to circumcision (see poem 11).

# I

"...and the garden with fiery swords"—See Gen 3:24: "So He drove out the man; and He placed at the east of the garden of Eden the cherubim, and the flaming sword which turned every way, to keep the way to the tree of life." For other possible allusions to the Garden of Eden see poems 4 and 8.

"...and heaven and earth with a word"—This is a reference to the creation that came to be through God's word in Genesis chapter 1. In Christianity the word (*logos*) is a synonym for Jesus, according to John 1:1–5: "In the beginning was the Word, and the Word was with God, and the Word was God. He was with God in the beginning. Through him all things were made; without him nothing was made that has been made. In him was life, and that life was the light of all mankind. The light shines in the darkness, and the darkness has not overcome it." See also poem 32.

"Blessed are you who binds the arm to the heart"—This can be an allusion to the *Teffilin* (phylacteries) which observant Jews put on their forehead and arm during the morning prayer on weekdays, based on the verse in Deut 11:18: "Therefore shall you lay up these My words in your heart and in your soul; and you shall bind them for a sign upon your hand, and they shall be for frontlets between your eyes." The one for the hand is tied on the inside of the left arm, next to the heart. Cohen mentioned in an interview that he resumed this practice a few years prior to the publishing of the book.[48] The *Teffilin* are also alluded to below in poem 19, and mentioned once literally in poem 22. The binding of the heart to the arm can also signify the willingness to act upon what the heart feels, the unifying of intention and action towards the mending of the self and the world.

"... and the will to the will"—On the two types of the will according to Cohen see the notes for poem 4.

"Who has written a name on a gate, that she might find it, and come into my room"—This alludes to the next verse but one, Deut 11:20: "And you shall write them upon the door-posts of your house, and upon your gate," which is the origin of the custom of the Mezuzah that Jews nail to the doorposts of their houses. The

---

48. Kurzweil, "I *Am* the Little Jew Who Wrote the Bible," 384.

"she" here, as usual, has a double meaning: either spiritual (the Torah, "Understanding"), or erotic (a lover).

**"Who defends a heart with strangerhood"**—The last word might be Cohen's original creation, perhaps having to do with his fear of commitment, but also with the position of the artist as sometimes a stranger in the world. See also the reference to "The Stranger Song" under poem 2, and the poems and song lyrics collection *Stranger Music*.

## 15

This short poem seems to offer a second climax in the process of reconnecting with the tradition. The speaker feels like a part of the community using the plural form "we" and stating **"How beautiful our heritage"** (see also poems 5 and 6). However, this feeling is not unequivocal as seen in the following poems, and even at this peak, paradoxically, solitude is still the preferable state for being in contact with the divine, here once again identified as "the Name." It is also possible that "solitude" hints at the exile (see poem 24).

**"We stand in rags"**—See the notes on the fourth verse of the song "If It Be Your Will" under poem 4 above.

**"... how bountiful this solitude"**—"Solitude" is one of those words Cohen makes a special use of both in this book (see also poems 34, 36, 39, 47, and 48), and elsewhere in his poetry and songs; see, for example, the song "Our Lady of Solitude" on the album *Recent Songs* (1979), or the line "And I love your solitude, I love your pride" in "Joan of Arc" on his third album, *Songs of Love and Hate* (1971). And as said above, solitude can be an asset when seeking the divine.

**"... we beg for tears to dissolve the immovable landmarks of hatred"**—In continuing a theme from the previous poem, this may be a wish for the end of hatred between the children of Abraham.

**"... from which all things arise in splendour, depending one upon the other"**—Another allusion to the emanation of the *sefirot*, as also depicted in the *Zohar, The Book of Splendor*.

# I

"Splendour" is also the common translation of the name of the eighth *sefira* (*Hod*).

## 16

After reaching a certain peak, the speaker's soul descends again into suffering and pain. Loneliness is mentioned here, rather than solitude.

**"Return, spirit, to this lowly place"**—This must have been inspired, paradoxically, by Ps 116:7: "Return, O my soul, to your rest; for the Lord has dealt bountifully with you," although here there is no return to rest but rather to a lowly place and in particular to loneliness. Still, through its descent the soul becomes better attuned to the message, so the suffering is not meaningless but perhaps elevating. In a more radical way, Cohen dealt with the idea of finding redemption through sin in his second novel, *Beautiful Losers* (1966).

**"Come down. There is no path where you project yourself"**—As mentioned more than once before, Cohen does not wish to reach the highest spheres, but rather remain firmly on earth, and he is warning his soul against the assent for which it is not suited.

**"You do not know how to bind your heart to the skylark"**—This may be an allusion to the poem "To a Skylark" by Percy Bysshe Shelley, in which the bird, characterized as "spirit," signifies happiness and in particular the art of poetry in its perfection.[49] The speaker here may be realizing that his ambition for creating great poetry and songs cannot yet be achieved and he needs to **"Kneel here, search here, with both hands . . ."**

**". . . the cat's cradle of your tiny distress"**—This image also appears in Cohen's first novel: "The telephone poles are playing intricate games of Cat's Cradle with the rushing wires."[50] Compare poem 23.

---

49. I am grateful to Louis Schwartz for suggesting this allusion.
50. Cohen, *The Favourite Game*, 95.

"**. . . the one who says, 'It is not good that man should be alone'**"—Quoting Gen 2:18, when God decided to create the woman to keep man company. Incidentally, leading Hebrew poet Nathan Zach's take on this verse was: "It is not good that man should be alone / but he is alone anyhow." Zach's poem was set to music by Matti Caspi, a leading Israeli composer, who accompanied Cohen on his guitar in the Sinai desert during the 1973 war. In his memoires Zach wrote that he met Cohen in Tel Aviv in the early 1960's, and gave him a bed for the night.

"**. . . so that when she appears, she will stand before you, not against you**"—The second half of the above verse from Genesis reads: "I will make him a help meet for him." In the original Hebrew "meet for him" is *kenegdo*, which is a stumbling block for translators as it can mean "in front of him," "opposite him," or even "against him." Cohen must have been familiar with the Midrash on this verse: "If he merits it—a helper, if not—against him" (Bereshit Rabbah 17:3; see also poem 37). Here the expression refers to the personification of loneliness, for which the speaker expresses longing.

"**. . . under the low-built shelter of repentance**"—For "shelter" see poem 41; for "repentance" see poems 32, 34, and 42.

## 17

Can the tradition indeed be the right answer? The speaker criticizes those who observe it although having lost its essence or meaning. Cohen had already done so in his early work. Both his first novel *The Favourite Game* and his second collection of poetry *The Spice-Box of Earth*, with poems such as "Brighter than Our Sun" and "Priests 1957,"[51] contain some biting criticism of those who pray out of habit without giving true meaning to their prayer. Still, the speaker in this poem does not lose hope of finding refuge in prayer, even when he seems in danger of losing himself in a confusion of false identities.

---

51. Cohen, *The Spice-Box of Earth*, 53; 69.

I

"... the minor singers, the second-rate priests"—Here Cohen is using sarcasm and irony directed at himself and his family members undisguisedly.

"Let the light catch the thread from which the man is hanging . . . O single strand of spittle glistening"—These images may originate in a well-known traditional Buddhist story, which was also adapted by the Japanese writer Ryūnosuke Akutagawa and translated into English; in it Buddha lowers a shining spider thread into Hell in order to save one sinner, but when that man, on seeing others following him and climbing up the thread shouts at them to climb down, the thread snaps and he falls back down.

"Our Lady of the Torah"—Mixing the Christian title associated with Mary mother of Jesus in the various forms in which she is venerated, such as "Our Lady of the Harbour" mentioned in the song "Suzanne" on Cohen's first album, with the Jewish "Torah," which is often personified in female form throughout the book (see poems 3, 5, and 11).

"Angel of Darkness"—After his fall, Lucifer, the shining angel (see poem 8), turned into the angel of Darkness (see also poem 49).

"...the difference between a palace and a cave"—The king's palace was alluded to in the first poems, although not mentioned literally; for "cave" see poem 25. The combination of nouns also brings to mind once again the life-story of King David, who on escaping from King Saul's palace hid in a cave (1 Sam 24).

## 18

The reality depicted in this poem which reads like a short story—one of several poems in the book that do not constitute a prayer, although they may include a prayerful element—partially reflects southern France, where Cohen spent time during the writing of his book, but also other places such as Montreal's immigrant district where he had an apartment during his adult years. It may also have something of Hydra, the Greek island on which he bought his first house.

"... the Romans, their triumph, and the tiny thorn in their side that we represent"—The Romans here represent the Christian Church, for which the Jews remained a "tiny thorn" in its side. Simultaneously it can refer to the historical Romans of antiquity against whom the Jews rebelled several times, mixing the present with the past. For another variation—a story of the past which partially represents the present—see poem 25.

"Our children go to the Roman schools"—In reality Cohen's children were educated locally in France and did not receive a Jewish education.[52]

"... and we hope that the grandchildren will return to us"—It is typical of immigrant communities that the first generation, immigrating as adults, work hard but cannot fully assimilate into their new society. Their children want very much to assimilate, want nothing to do with their parents' heritage, and are even ashamed of their habits and of the broken way they speak the local language. The grandchildren are already total natives of the new country, but if the grandparents are still around as relics from the Old Country, they may take some interest in learning about their heritage.

"Take heart, you who were born in captivity of a fixed predicament..."—The "short story" ends with a prophetic warning: the speaker offers encouragement to the exiled, followed by a warning to the strong and mighty whose power is but an illusion. This is one of several cases in this book, as well as in his songs and other work, where Cohen moves beyond the personal to the political or social reality.

## 19

This poem combines thanksgiving with a plea for help. The motif of language stands out here, including the ability to speak and to sing, and to hear the other, in spite of all the suffering. The teacher is mentioned again, but Cohen's grandfather, who was also one of

---

52. Simmons, *I'm Your Man*, 310.

I

his teachers, is mentioned here literally for the first and only time (see the notes for poem 13).

"**You draw the tears back to my eyes**"—For tears see poem 12.

"**. . . the mountain of your word**"—About "word" see poem 14.

"**. . . you bound my arm with my grandfather's strength**"—This must be another allusion to the *Teffilin* (see poem 14).

"**. . . unspeakable explanation of the smoke and cruelty**"—This is most likely a reference to the Holocaust (see notes for poem 12). The Holocaust is mentioned literally once in the song "The Captain" on the *VP* album, and is often referenced in other poems, songs and prose work by Cohen. The explanation is "unspeakable" because something like the Holocaust cannot be explained or given any theological justification, but the speaker still wishes to maintain hope.

"**. . . let me dare the boldness of joy**"—The speaker feels that joy requires boldness, because of the endless suffering in the world. Privately, it requires a strong effort to overcome depression. "Joy" or "joyous" appear only twice more in the book (see poems 33 and 38).


20

This poem reads like an extension of the previous one, expounding both suffering and hope. The theme of language appears here too (through the mention of the **Tower of Babel**). Poems 19 and 20 differ from the previous and following poems, 18 and 21, both of which are written like short "stories."

"**Like an unborn infant swimming to be born**"—This is paralleled in the song "Dance Me to the End of Love" on the *VP* album: "Dance me to the children who are asking to be born." Other words or expressions from the song have parallels in this poem such as "beauty" or "Babylon" ("Babel" here). This line also brings to mind the one from "Like a Bird on a Wire" on Cohen's second album: "Like a baby stillborn." See also the quote from "Stories of the Street" under poem 30.

"**. . . the scorn of my enemy**"—Various biblical references are possible here, for example Ps 42:10: "Why hast Thou forgotten me? Why go I mourning under the oppression of the enemy?" (see also poems 10, 27, and 39).

"**O king of absolute unity**"—The absolute oneness and unity of God is, of course, a basic principle of Judaism, but it is possible that Cohen had some specific verses in mind, such as the words of the prophet, Zech 14:9: "And the Lord shall be King over all the earth; In that day shall the Lord be One, and His name one." Another possible allusion is the popular *Yigdal* ("Magnify") hymn, sung at the synagogue on various occasions, the second verse of which reads: "He is One—and there is no unity like His Oneness—Inscrutable and infinite is His Oneness." The speaker here, who knows only relative or incomplete unity in his life, yearns for an absolute one. The expression "Lord of Unity" appears in poem 22 ("unity" appears also in poems 29 and 39; the verb "unifies" in poems 42, 47, and 50).

"**. . . king . . . ape . . .**"—See poem 2. There are two mentions of apes in this poem: as a group—"**apes come down from the Tower of Babel**"—which must refer to humanity at large and hints at the use of language or languages (Gen 11:7–9), and as a private individual: "**but in my heart an ape sees the beauty bathing**"; this latter one parallels the unruly ape of poem 2, symbolizing the vulgar parts of the psyche, or the "evil inclination." For the "beauty bathing" see poem 7 and the song "Hallelujah" on the *VP* album.

"**O shield of Abraham**"—From the *'Amidah* prayer: "O King, a helper, a savior and a shield. Blessed are you, Lord, Shield of Abraham," which in turn is based on Gen 15:1: "After these things the word of the Lord came unto Abram in a vision, saying: Fear not, Abram, I am your shield. . ." For "shield" see also poem 4.

## 21

Like poem 18, this too is a kind of "short story." The teacher here is clearly Roshi (see poem 2). The speaker expresses his frustration with the practice of Zen meditation and depicts his teacher as

# I

intimidating, but also as the one who ultimately helped him find his own way.

**"My teacher gave me what I do not need, told me what I need not know"**—This poem, like in a few earlier cases, refers to the absurd side in the spirit of Zen and to the difficulties on the path of practice. Cohen often said that he did not come to Zen to seek any knowledge, but to be close to Roshi.

**"He referred me to the crickets when I had to sing"**—Crickets often appear in Cohen's songs and poems; a well-known example is "Summer Haiku":

> Silence
> and a deeper silence
> when the crickets
> hesitate[53]

Crickets also appear in the song "Night Comes On" on the *VP* album. But here Cohen must have had in mind the passage titled "Formal in his Thought of her" from his book *Death of a Lady's Man*.[54] In this passage the two are listening to the crickets on Mt. Baldy when Roshi suggests that Cohen write a poem about them. Cohen says that he has already done so, and then Roshi himself offers three poems about crickets in broken English. The passage ends with Roshi telling Cohen: "You should write more sad." In another version of this suggestion, Roshi, who was present at some of the recordings of Cohen's fourth album, told him: "You should sing more sad."[55]

**". . . I swelled without filling"**—See in poem 2, where the speaker expanded and gave birth to an ape.

**". . . that realm where I barked with a dog"**—The short poem "Roshi" in *Book of Longing* reads as follows:

---

53. Cohen, *The Spice-Box of Earth*, 68.
54. Cohen, *Death of a Lady's Man*, 171–72, retitled "Roshi" in Cohen, *Stranger Music*, 275–76.
55. Simmons, *I'm Your Man*, 267.

> I never really understood
> what he said
> but every now and then
> I find myself
> barking with the dog
> or bending with the irises
> or helping out
> in other little ways[56]

**"He suffered me to play at friendship with my truest friend. When he was certain that I was incapable of self-reform, he flung me across the fence of the Torah"**—The dictum: "Make a fence for the Torah" is taken from Mishnah, tractate Avot (known in English also as "Ethics of the Fathers" or "Sayings of the Jewish Fathers") 1:1. A similar dictum also appears in 3:13: "Tradition is a safeguarding fence around Torah." The idea is to put a "fence" before the edge of the Law, before its most extreme implication, in order to prevent people from failing to keep the Torah (see also poem 14). The former sentence here may be connected with the poem "One of My Letters":

> I corresponded with a famous rabbi
> but my teacher caught sight of one of my letters
> and silenced me.
> "Dear Rabbi," I wrote him for the last time,
> "I do not have the authority or understanding
> To speak of these matters.
> I was just showing off.
> Please forgive me.
> Your Jewish brother,
> Jikan Eliezer."[57]

Cohen demonstrates here once again the admixture in his life of Jewish faith and Zen practice, and as mentioned in the Introduction, he often said that the one enhanced the other in his life. So, when he is being flung across the fence of the Torah, the direction would be inward rather than outward. "Jikan" is the Buddhist

---

56. Cohen, *Book of Longing*, 16.
57. Cohen, *Book of Longing*, 5.

I

name given to Cohen by Roshi, while "Eliezer" (meaning "God is my help") is the Hebrew name given to him at his birth.

22

This poem offers familiar self-deprecation, but not without humor. Also familiar is the final request for help (as in poem 17).

"**He's working hard, dragging that donkey up Mount Moriah**"—This is another indirect reference to the story of the binding of Isaac (see poem 10). Mount Moriah is "the place" where Abraham brought his son Isaac to be sacrificed, and which was identified in later Jewish tradition with Temple Mount in Jerusalem. Intentionally or inadvertently, this poem is numbered 22, the same number of the chapter in the Book of Genesis where this story is told. The hard work can refer to either or all of the speaker's efforts to maintain the tradition, to meditate in Zen, or to do his daily work.

"**. . . the authentic muffled cry of his heart, so thoroughly documented and unattended**"—The muffled cry can be Abraham's, Isaac's, or the speaker's. His cries are documented but the suffering is not cured.

"**Bring a mirror, let him see the monkey struggling with the black tefillin straps**"—See poem 2, and the passage about Roshi quoted there, which also mentions a mirror. This is the only time the *Tefillin* are mentioned literally after having been alluded to in poems 14 and 19. In this poem both the stubborn donkey and the unruly monkey symbolize the vulgar part of the psyche with which the speaker feels a constant need to struggle in spite of his repeated failures (see also poem 20).

"**Lord of Unity**"—See poem 20.

"**. . . the wedding with no blood**"—A possible association is to *Blood Wedding* (*Bodas de sangre*), the 1932 play by Federico Garcia Lorca, whose work was one of Cohen's major poetic inspirations ever since his youth.[58] The play tells the tragic story of a wedding

---

58. Simmons, *I'm Your Man*, 28–29.

disrupted by passion and violence rooted in a family feud. Cohen named his daughter after the Spanish poet, and turned one of his poems into the song "Take this Waltz" (originally, *Pequeño vals vienés*), on his *I'm Your Man* album. In fact, that song appeared earlier as the first track on the tribute album *Poetas en Nueva York*, released in Spain in 1986 on the fiftieth anniversary of Lorca's death. On his posthumous album, *Thanks for the Dance* (2019), there is an English version of another Lorca poem, "The Night of Santiago" (originally, *La casada infiel*).

**23**

Like poem 18, this one is also a "short story," revolving around the Jewish minority in a Christian world and the notion of exile. In the last sentence the speaker is identified as one of the poor, as well as the strangers, but even in this condition he can expect **"the unimagined charities of accident."**

**"My sister and I being estranged"**—The poem later reveals that the "sister" here is probably a metaphor for Christianity. In spite of the common origin, the Christian Church and the Jewish people became estranged and hostile to each other.

**"I parked my trailer at the furthest limit of her fields"**—The trailer is taken from reality at the time of the book's writing, although it was parked outside the house occupied by Cohen's children and former partner, not his sister. It also hints at the "Wandering Jew" motif, which in Cohen's work is often coupled with or replaced by the Gypsy, usually in the context of the Holocaust, for example: "I sing this for the Jews and the Gypsies and the smoke that they made" in "Please Don't Pass Me By (A Disgrace)" on his first live album (1973), and many years later: "I listen to their story / Of the Gypsies and the Jews" in "Almost Like the Blues" on the *Popular Problems* album (2014). Cohen may also have absorbed the Gypsy motif due to Lorca's influence; see in particular the song "The Gypsy's Wife" on the *Recent Songs* album (1979), and also the lines: "I used to think I was some kind of Gypsy boy / before I let you take me home" in "So Long Marianne" on his first album. In

I

reality Cohen also wandered a lot, having lived at different times on and off in Montreal, New York, London, Hydra, Nashville, Paris and Los Angeles, on top of his arduous tours around the world.

"... the corner that is left, by law, to the poor"—See Lev 19:9–10; also 23:22: "And when you reap the harvest of your land, you shall not wholly reap the corner of your field, neither shall you gather the gleaning of your harvest; you shall leave them for the poor, and for the stranger: I am the Lord your God."

"It was a Saturday"—The Jewish Sabbath; see the early poem "After the Sabbath Prayers."[59]

"Let your sister, with her towers and gardens, praise the incomparable handiwork of the Lord, but you are pledged to the breath of the Name"—The "sister," or the Christian majority, has the land and praises the Lord through the construction of great edifices and beautiful gardens, but for the Jews all that is left is reciting prayers; even here Cohen combines the Name with breathing that has to do with Zen, but also with Kabbalistic images (see the notes for poem 7).

**24**

This is one of the longest poems in the book (poem 27 is a little longer). The speaker returns here to the feelings of depression, suffering and sin depicted in previous poems (see poems 12 and 16). Besides the private pain, which is expressed once again in a new way, and the hope of gaining forgiveness and redemption, the political-historical aspect is also brought up, and will stand out more strongly in some poems in the second part of the book (see poem 27). The request for personal redemption widens out into a plea for global redemption from the nightmare of war and human cruelty which manifests itself in an endless circle of revenge. Several key words are repeated in this poem, including "name," "law," and "mercy."

59. Cohen, *The Spice-Box of Earth*, 2.

"**O draw me out of an easy skill into the art of the holy**"—A touching request coming from an artist who was known for his scrupulous efforts to find the correct expression. Here he wishes to elevate his work into the sphere of holiness.

"**. . . my word for the day of atonement forgotten**"—As in other cases in this book, Cohen sometimes uses lower case when upper case is expected (here in the English title for *Yom Kippur*), perhaps wishing to make it either more general (not exclusively Jewish) or more personal (his own day of atonement). The "word" here could be the holy name of God (YHWH), which the high priest would only utter during the temple rituals on the Day of Atonement. See also under poem 6.

"**Lift me up with a new heart**"—See Ezek 36:26: "A new heart also will I give you, and a new spirit will I put within you; and I will take away the stony heart out of your flesh, and I will give you a heart of flesh."

"**. . . for my father's sake**"—The father is usually mentioned in the book in connection with keeping the tradition: see also poems 5 and 38. In poem 12, "father of mercy" is one of a chain of titles for God.

"**. . . through worlds destroyed and worlds to come**"—This is a reference to the Midrash (Bereshit Rabba 3:7): "God created worlds and destroyed them before he created the current ones." This was further developed in the Kabbalah. The future worlds are the ones following the completion of the mending process.

"**. . . the bomb falls on the pilot's son**"—Our acts put the next generation in danger; it is possible that this image occurred to Cohen in association with the 1964 American film *Fail-Safe*, in which a pilot is required to drop an atomic bomb on the city where his sons live.

"**. . . the riot shouts out to be calmed**"—It seems that the speaker suspects the sincerity of violent protests; alternatively, the riot may have become a cry of anguish that wishes to be calmed.

"**. . . the general exile thickens**"—"Exile" is mentioned literally in the book only a few times (see also poems 7 and 34, and "exiles" in poem 18). As the scion of East-European Jewish

# I

families of immigrants to Christian North America—his father's family had lived in Canada for several generations, but his mother Masha still spoke English with a Russian accent—who grew up with the awareness of the Holocaust, the idea of "exile" must have been familiar to Cohen. Here he gives "exile" a general meaning, the feeling of the soul being exiled in this world which it inhabits for a mere moment as he says at the end of the poem, especially when considering God's absence (in the following). In fact, "exile" has a deeper existential meaning, because according to the myth of the Lurianic Kabbalah with which Cohen was familiar, the contraction of God himself in order to vacate space for creation constitutes a form of exile. It follows that exile is the fundamental status of being to which only the remote messianic expectations may offer a solution.

"**. . . the whole world becomes the memory of your absence**"—This absence was first expressed metaphorically in poem 1. The current sentence and the following ones express a messianic desire for redemption which will occur with the reaffirmation of the source of mercy to the world.

"**Now that all men hear each other**"—This was written in 1984, when the current accessibility of instant global communication and interaction was yet unimaginable. Still, even then, through the use of communication satellites, there was palatable progress compared with a decade or two earlier (in 1986 Paul Simon declared ironically on his album *Graceland*: "These are the days of miracle and wonder / This is the long distance call / The way the camera follows us in slo-mo / The way we look to us all").

"**. . . and count us back to the safety of your law, father of mercy, bride of the captured earth**"—Once again the speaker wishes to find safety under the wings of the tradition and the law. "Bride" is one of the images of *Malchut*, the tenth *sefirah*, and of the Sabbath. This image reappears in poem 35, there with a capital letter. Bride and groom also appear in poem 30, but in a different context; see also poem 29.

## 25

Like poems 18 and 23, this one is also written as a short "story," and in this case even as a legend. The material is taken from the past, but with relevance to the present. As in the previous poems, the personal and the general, the intimate family and global politics are woven together, but the seriousness is mixed with the humorous.

"**My son and I lived in a cave for many years**"—The poem begins with a variation on a well-known Talmudic anecdote, according to which the second century CE sage Rabbi Shimon bar Yochai and his son Elazar spent thirteen years in a cave in the Galilee hiding from the Romans (b. Shabbat 33b). Tradition attributes to Rabbi Shimon the compiling of Kabbalah's major work, *The Book of Splendor*, which was in fact compiled in Spain in the thirteenth century.

"'**I've had enough**'"—Cohen may have had a premonition when he wrote this in 1984. Years later, on Mt. Baldy, he too would come to the point when he'd say "I've had enough," and come down from the mountain.

"**My wife came back to me one strange afternoon, all changed, all lightened**"—This must be a piece of wishful thinking, expressing the hope of reviving the family after it had broken up. However, the speaker is aware that this can only happen under some "strange," dream-like circumstances, and that the wife will have to be "changed" and "lightened" (apparently, the whole blame lies with her in this case, as she is the one who is expected to change, although he is often willing to find fault with himself too). Later he also expresses the fear of being estranged from his children, although in the idyllic atmosphere of this particular poem, this obstacle is also surmounted.

"**. . . small bilingual editions of the Book of Psalms**"—Such books are sold as souvenirs for tourists in many places in the Holy Land. This is the only literal mention of the Book of Psalms, whose language and modes of expression are such an important part of *Book of Mercy*.

# I

"... **a goldsmith, a maker of ceremonial objects**"—This is part of the idyllic picture painted here, but two external associations may also be relevant. One is to the title of Cohen's second poetry book *The Spice-Box of Earth*: a spice-box is a Jewish ceremonial object used in the *Havdalah*, the ceremony that ends the Sabbath. The second has to do with the short poem appended at the end of this prose poem, which begins with "**Jerusalem of blood.**" This is an ironic variation on "Jerusalem of Gold," which is the name of a very famous modern Hebrew song. The item in the song, in turn, referred originally to a piece of jewelry mentioned in the Talmud, probably a golden brooch or a diadem in the shape of a city wall. There is a traditional anecdote according to which Rabbi Akiva, who was the teacher of the above-mentioned Rabbi Shimon bar Yochai, gave such an item to his wife on returning to her after long years of separation (b. Nedarim 50a).

"... **we gather at midnight before the Wall**"—The Wall, obviously, is the Western Wall in Jerusalem. There is a custom, originated in the Kabbalah, to mourn the destruction of the temple and the exile of God's presence at midnight (*Tikkun Chatzot*).

"... **the Romans do not eat flesh torn from a living animal**"—This refers to one of the "Seven Laws of Noah." In Judaism it is believed that only Jews are called upon to observe all the commandments of the Torah, traditionally numbered at 613, but gentiles too are expected to observe at least seven basic commandments which were concluded by the rabbis from Gen 9, where some but not all seven are literally mentioned. One of these commandments is to not be cruel to animals by eating part of a creature which is still alive. The "Romans" are mentioned here because the story supposedly takes place during the time of the Sages, but it also has a contemporary relevance, as in poem 18.

"**and the Christians are a branch of the tree**"—Cohen demonstrated here, as in other places in this book and elsewhere, his inclusive position.

"**and the apostate Jews are still embraced by the Word**"—A common Jewish saying, based on a Talmudic passage (b. Sanhedrin

44a) is: "a Jew, even having sinned, is still considered a Jew." For "the Word" see poem 14.

"... **we sing the time-honoured songs, and we compose new ones, as we were commanded**"—Here Cohen specifically ties the traditional liturgy with the contemporary one, of which he is one of the creators.

"***Let the nations rejoice / Jerusalem has been destroyed***"—The idyllic poem ends on a much more somber note with this appendix. The little poem at the end refers to the complicated admixture of religion and politics for which Jerusalem is notorious. "Jerusalem" is not only the real city, but also the utopic vision, "New Jerusalem," aspired to by various ideologies, here symbolized by Washington and Moscow, the leaders of the two main competing ideologies of the time. Cohen quoted here one part of Ps 67:5: "O let the nations be glad and sing for joy; for You will judge the peoples with equity, and lead the nations upon earth. Selah." Ironically, all ideologies have failed and the New Jerusalem cannot be realized, but still everyone is happy. See also the early poem "Isaiah" which describes the illusion of a perfectly happy reality, the very one against which the prophet is rising: "Why did Isaiah rage and cry, / Jerusalem is ruined, / your cities are burned with fire?"[60] The last line is a quote from Isa 1:7, although the prophet does not mention Jerusalem specifically here, as did Cohen a line earlier.

## 26

This short poem, which concludes the first part of the book, combines the description of meditation or guided imagery with the wish to find valuable artistic expression, which is one of the things that Cohen was trying to do in his book.

"**Sit in the chair and keep still. Let the dancer's shoulders emerge from your shoulders . . .**"—The speaker may not be able to dance, but he is imagining himself as "the dancer." In poem 10 he spoke about dancing with a broken knee. Dances and dancing

---

60. Cohen, *The Spice-Box of Erath*, 73.

# I

often appear in the work of Cohen, who seems to have been particularly enamored with the waltz. He may also have been thinking of the following lines from William Butler Yeats, one of the poets he greatly admired, which is the final stanza of "Among School Children":[61]

> Labour is blossoming or dancing where
> The body is not bruised to pleasure soul,
> Nor beauty born out of its own despair,
> Nor blear-eyed wisdom out of midnight oil.
> O chestnut tree, great rooted blossomer,
> Are you the leaf, the blossom or the bole?
> O body swayed to music, O brightening glance,
> How can we know the dancer from the dance?[62]

"... a clear song to which the dancer moves"—Beginning with poem 1, singing seems to be the way by which the speaker wishes to express himself (see also in poems 4, 10, 12, 16, 25, 28, 29, and 42). The ideal is that it will **"serve God in beauty."** This is significant also because it is the first time that capitalized "God" appears in the book; the second time is in the following poem, 27. Uncapitalized "god" appeared once before, in poem 10. Cohen must have used it sparingly and carefully in order to avoid blasphemy or sound too pretentious. Eventually the dancer is able to move. This may bring to mind once again King David who danced frantically in front of God in spite of his wife's scorn (2 Sam 6:14–23).

"... even a bitter man can praise Creation"—In poem 12 the speaker was raging about the beauty of the world viewed against a background of horror and suffering, but here he expresses reconciliation and the willingness to adhere to beauty in spite of everything. The rage in poem 12 was also against God (mentioned only as "you"), while here there is willingness to celebrate God in beauty, in the spirit of the hymns of the Psalms, which will reappear in the second part of the book (see poem 28, and more conspicuously, 29).

---

61. I am grateful to Louis Schwartz for suggesting this quote
62. Pethica, *Yeats's Poetry, Drama, and Prose,* 97–98.

# II

THE BOOK IS DIVIDED asymmetrically, and the second part opens with poem 27. Why does the first part end with poem 26? Since Cohen included exactly fifty numbered poems in the book, fifty being the number of his years of life when it was published, it might be supposed that he divided the book thus because he felt he had crossed a significant threshold in his life at twenty six. Indeed, 1960, the year when he reached that age, was the year when he started living on the Greek island of Hydra where he bought his first house,[63] met Marianne Ihlen who was to become his companion for the coming decade, completed his second poetry book, and made progress with the first novel he was to publish. In short, this year marked the beginning of his adult life. And as shown earlier, some poem numbers such as 9 and 13 may also carry significant meaning connected with the author's life. There could, of course, be other reasons for the particular division of the book (see also under I above).

## 27

The speaker's voice changes temporarily from that of the Psalmist to that of the admonishing prophet, in the vein of Amos or Isaiah. He protests against the wrong done in the name of nationalism all

---

63. Simmons, *I'm Your Man*, 81.

over the world, rebukes and demands justice. This criticism was already voiced earlier (see poem 24 and the final lines of poem 25), but here it is much more forceful and direct. The prophetic, admonishing style also appeared occasionally in a political context in Cohen's songs, such as "The Story of Isaac" (see poems 4 and 10), and several songs on the album *The Future* (1992), such as "Democracy," "Anthem" and the title song, as well as in his poetry.

"**Israel**"—Here it refers to the biblical People of Israel who created the tradition to which contemporary Jewish people are the heirs, and not specifically the State of Israel although it is also included.

"**. . . the Church that calls itself Israel**"—The Christian church traditionally sees itself as the rightful heir to the covenant between God and Israel (the "New Testament" is in fact the "New Covenant"), and sometimes regraded itself as "spiritual Israel" as opposing "Israel according to the flesh," in a doctrine known as "Supersessionism."

"**. . . none of these lands is yours**"—This line—together with "**Therefore the lands belong to none of you**" and "**To every people the land is given on condition**" further down—is based on the biblical notion that the land belongs to God, while human beings' dwelling on it is conditional. This is particularly relevant to the Promised Land and the People of Israel, as in Lev 25:23: "And the land shall not be sold in perpetuity; for the land is Mine; for you are strangers and settlers with Me" (see also Deut 28). However, the speaker here applies this notion to all nations and all lands indiscriminately, and this inclusiveness may also have its seeds in the Bible. For example, Deut 32:8 says: "When the Most High gave to the nations their inheritance, when He separated the children of men," a notion clearly reflected in this poem. The biblical prophets widened the scope further so that even nations which did not enter a personal covenant with God as did the people of Israel, would be punished by the loss of their lands for their bloodthirstiness and lack of righteousness; see particularly Isa 13–23, Ezek 25–36, and Amos 1–2.

**"Ishmael"**—In poem 14 he was portrayed more favorably, but here he is one of those who are to blame, including Israel.

**"Perceived or not, there is a covenant"**—Apart from the particular covenant between God and Israel, the Hebrew Bible recognizes a more inclusive one made with all humanity as specified in Gen 9:1–17. Hence the idea of the "Seven Laws of Noah" (see the notes for poem 25). The speaker here is following all these biblical passages in arguing that the world belongs to God, and human beings are his mere lodgers who are supposed to follow his rules. Breaking the covenant will lead to punishment, even when it is not recognized or understood, as in the following **"have you not noticed that the world has been taken away?"**[64]

**"You have no place"**—See the discussion of "place" in the notes for poem 8.

**"Because you do not wrestle with your angel... Because your cowardice has led you to believe that the victor does not limp"**—This is an obvious reference to the story of Jacob in Gen 32:24–32 which was previously hinted at in poem 10, and the struggle from which he came out limping. In the biblical text, Jacob wrestles literally with "a man," but this figure was turned into an angel in later interpretations, and already in the Bible itself, in Hos 12:5. Another common interpretation is that Jacob wrestled with God himself. The speaker says that although the struggle cannot end without injury or pain, it is indispensable, and those who avoid it live without God. Incidentally, in Rembrandt's depiction of the scene, in an oil painting which is now in Berlin's Gemäldegalerie, the struggle looks more like a love-act between the masculine Jacob and the feminine angel. In his genius Rembrandt was able to depict in one scene both the Christian concept of God's unconditional love, and the Jewish thinking since Abraham, which is alluded to in this poem, that a struggle with God must not be avoided.

---

64. For more on Cohen's view of the covenant, and other crucial aspects of his work, see Pally.

## 28

Following the fiery prophetic language of the previous poem, this one returns to the style of the Psalms and the language of the *Siddur*. "Mercy," "name," and "song" are once again key words.

"... **let me study your ways which are just beyond the hope of evil**"—This line is an amalgamation of various biblical verses, including Moses' words when entreating God in Exod 33:13: "Now therefore, I pray Thee, if I have found grace in Thy sight, show me now Thy ways, that I may know Thee." Also Ps 25:4: "Show me Thy ways, O Lord; teach me Thy paths," and Ps 27:11: "Teach me Thy way, O Lord; and lead me in an even path, because of them that lie in wait for me." Prov 10:28: "The hope of the righteous is gladness; but the expectation of the wicked shall perish." The speaker seems to imply that goodness is absolute in a way which evil cannot attain.

"... **whose mercy is to be the secret of longing**"—The heart's longing is to be based on the feeling that there is a source of mercy. The speaker here wishes to reassure himself and be freed from misleading thoughts. "Longing" is another particularly meaningful word for Cohen, repeated about ten times in this book (poems 14, 16, 29, 30, 31, 35, and 36) and serves in the title of his following one.

"... **let us bring to you the sorrows of our freedom**"—Free will is necessary (see poems 4 and 29), but it can also be a burden; "freedom" was mentioned once before in poem 6.

"**Blessed are you, who opens a gate in every moment**"—On the opening of gates see the notes for poem 5.

"... **who have broken down your world to gather hearts**"—The speaker returns here to the Kabbalistic idea of the broken world; see under poems 1 and 10. However, here he is referring more specifically to the human realm: brokenness leads to the opening of the heart (see also poem 24).

"**Blessed is your name, blessed is the confession of your name**"—Once again reflecting the language of the *Shema* (see poem 6): "Blessed be the name of the glory of His kingdom for ever and ever."

**"Arouse my heart again with the limitless breath you breath into me"**—See "master of my breath" in poem 7 and the notes there, and the quote from Gen 2:7 under poem 13.

## 29

A particularly long poem, rich in images, in which the speaker picks up the style and language of the Psalms even more markedly than in the previous poem. He also follows the way of Midrash: using parts of verses to create something new and unique. The speaker addresses his soul so it will turn to the source of mercy out of the willingness to be judged.

**"Bless the Lord, O my soul"**—The source here are Pss 103 and 104; the former focuses on God's mercy and grace and on his reign over heaven and earth, while the latter praises God as the creator and sustainer of the universe. The phrase "Bless the Lord, O my soul" is repeated at the beginning and the end of each of the two psalms as it is in this poem.

**". . . who made you a singer in his holy house forever"**—See poem 1. The Levites were the singers in the temple rather than the priests (*kohanim*), but the singing suggests continuity from one generation to the next, and in the synagogue the whole community sings in unison. In *Book of Longing* Cohen included a self-portrait under which he inscribed four words in Hebrew taken from a verse in the *Shema*, recited in the morning prayer right after the Holiness Verse (see poem 1); the translation is: "They chant sweet melodies to the blessed God."[65] Cohen also added some English text to the drawing, saying: "just to have been one of them, even on the lowest rung," which could refer to the rungs of the ladder which the angels climb while praising God (combining Gen 28:12 and Isa 6:1–2). It could also refer to the priests at the time of the temple. This line may also allude to Ps 23:6: "And I shall dwell in the house of the Lord for ever."

---

65. Cohen, *Book of Longing*, 36.

# II

"... **who has given you a tongue like the wind, and a heart like the sea**"—Both the wind and the sea are conspicuous images in Pss 103 & 104, and Cohen used them in the spirit of the Midrash to create new images.

"... **who has journeyed you from generation to generation**"—This can refer to the reincarnation of the soul, an idea that entered Judaism relatively late through the Kabbalah, or simply to the idea of tradition which is carried on and handed down from one generation to the next.

"... **to this impeccable moment of sweet bewilderment**"—For bewilderment—which is here defined as "sweet," perhaps because it leads to a longing for the clarity of the divine—see also poem 48, and the passage "Moving into a Period" in *Book of Longing*, a part of which was quoted under poem 6. It begins:

> We are moving into a period of bewilderment, a curious moment in which people find light in the midst of despair, and vertigo at the summit of their hopes. It is a religious moment also, and here is the danger. People will want to obey the voice of Authority, and many strange constructs of just what authority is will arise in every mind...[66]

"**Bless the Lord who has surrounded the traffic of human interest with the majesty of his law**"—"Law" is a major theme all along the book, alternating with "Torah." Unlike the Christian perspective, there is no conflict between "law" and "mercy" (see poems 17 and 24). On the contrary, the speaker's view is that the law is necessary for the human condition, no less so than mercy. The parallel on the *VP* album is the song "The Law" (see notes for poems 7 and 8).

"... **who has given a direction to the falling leaf, and a goal to the green shoot**"—For "leaf" see poem 3. This sentence is also reminiscent of the Midrash (Bereshit Rabbah 10:6) where it is said that not a green shoot ever grows without a star in heaven causing

---

66. Cohen, *Book of Longing*, 34.

it to grow, while in later versions "star" was replaced by an angel telling it to do so.

**"Tremble, my soul, before the one who creates good and evil, that a man may choose among worlds"**—This is based on Isa 45:7: "I form the light, and create darkness; I make peace, and create evil; I am the Lord, that does all these things," and on Deut 30:19: "I call heaven and earth to witness against you this day, that I have set before you life and death, the blessing and the curse; therefore choose life, that you may live, you and your seed." As mentioned earlier (poem 4), free choice is a major concept in Judaism, although it was recognized that it could be in conflict with God's omniscience. Rabbi Akiva declared in the Mishnah (Avot 3:15): "Everything is foreseen, and freewill is given, and with goodness the world is judged." So, even though "everything is foreseen," human beings still have a choice between doing right or wrong. The absence of free choice would make religious life meaningless.

**". . . until the time when he suspends his light and withdraws into himself, and there is no world, and there is no soul anywhere"**—See poem 1. The mending (*Tikkun*) will be complete with the return of all the sparks of divine light to their source, nullifying the created world.

**". . . those who say, I have not sinned"**—This may relate to the prayer of confession (*Viddui*), recited twice daily, which says in part: "Our God and God of our fathers, let our prayer come before you and do not ignore our supplication. For we are not so brazen-faced and stiff-necked to say to you, Lord, our God, and God of our fathers, 'We are righteous and have not sinned.' But, indeed, we and our fathers have sinned."

**"Gather me, O my soul, around your longing"**—As in the previous poem, longing for mercy is the focal point of the soul's movement.

**". . . who widens space with the thought of his name"**—This refers to the primordial space (called *tehiru* in the Lurianic Kabbalah) which appeared when the Godhead contracted itself to make space for the world.

# II

"**. . . cry out with tears and song and every instrument**"—See Ps 150:1–4: "Hallelujah, Praise God in His sanctuary . . . Praise Him with the blast of the horn; praise Him with the psaltery and harp. Praise Him with the timbrel and dance; praise Him with stringed instruments and the pipe . . ."

"**. . . stretch yourself toward the undivided glory which he established merely as his footstool**"—Following Ps 103:19: "The Lord has established His throne in the heavens and His kingdom rules over all," and Isa 66:1: "Thus says the Lord: Heaven is my throne and the earth is my footstool." In other cases the temple in Jerusalem, or more specifically the Arch of the Covenant within the temple, is called God's footstool (see Ps 132:7; 1 Chr 28:2).

"**. . . when he created forever . . . gates of return**"—The images here are again partially based on Ps 104. "Forever" could also refer to the seventh *sefira* (*Netzach*, usually translated "Eternity"). For "gates" see poem 28 (also poem 5); for "return" or "repentance" see also poems 16, 32, 34, and 42.

"**. . . and he made it-is-finished**"—This may be an allusion to Jesus whose last words were these, according to John 19:30. See an earlier possible reference to the Gospel According to John under poem 14. It may also allude to Gen 2:1: "And the heaven and the earth were finished, and all the host of them."

"**. . . the atoms of love**"—"Love" could allude to the fourth *sefira* (*Chesed*, also translated "Grace"), and see also poem 37. "Love" is mentioned in the book nearly twenty times (including in poems 1 and 49), and it is directed towards both an absolute reality and a temporal one. Indeed, the "holy house" mentioned at the beginning of the poem might also be interpreted as referring to the body in which the soul resides, and if so the poem could also have a sexual overtone. According to this reading, the "impeccable moment of sweet bewilderment" could refer to the moment of climax, and the following result is "that I may bring you forth." The combining of faith with erotic symbolism is common in various forms of the Jewish tradition, beginning with the allegorical interpretation of the biblical Song of Songs as alluding to the love between God and his people, and followed by the heavily erotic symbolism in the

*Zohar* and other branches of the Kabbalah. Cohen embraced this tradition which is manifest throughout his work.

## 30

Contrary to the conciliatory style of the previous two poems, this one describes ugly human reality in dark colors. The prophetic rage directed against political and social injustice in poem 27 is here directed against environmental destruction, among other sins. This is the closest Cohen comes in this book to portraying a dystopian reality.

**"The bride and the bridegroom sink down to combine, and flesh is brought forth as if it were child"**—This and other lines in this poem bring to mind Cohen's song "Stories Of The Street" from his first album, which uses somewhat similar language and subject matter with lines such as:

> The age of lust is giving birth, and both the parents ask
> the nurse to tell them fairy tales on both sides of the glass.
> And now the infant with his cord is hauled in like a kite,
> and one eye filled with blueprints, one eye filled with night.

However, in this song love is portrayed as a possible remedy, while in the poem there seems to be no hope at all as long as human beings continue on the same path, although hope can be found in the poems preceding and following this one.

**". . . as if they had washed their hands, as if they had lifted up their hands"**—The image of hand-washing may come from the New Testament (Matt 15:24), but it is also a daily ritualistic requirement followed by a specific blessing, obligatory for observant Jews. The hand-lifting is associated with the Priestly Blessing (*Birkat Kohanim*) with which Cohen was well-familiar and recited at the end of his concert in Ramat Gan, Israel in 2009 (see also poem 41).

**". . . the trees and waters hide themselves behind a blessing which they are too proud to know . . . There is no world without the blessing . . ."**—In Jewish tradition it is common to recite various blessings (*Berachot*) during the day, including before and after eating and on various other occasions, such as the handwashing mentioned above (see also the following).

"**. . . because there is no fence in their heart, nor knowledge of the one who varies the appearance of creatures**"—On "fence" as a required limit see poem 21. The speaker also alludes to one of the common Jewish blessings uttered on seeing a strange-looking human being or animal: "Blessed. . . Who makes creatures different" (Cohen gives a more literal English translation of the original Hebrew). Cohen was well aware of this blessing as he mentioned it in an interview. Here he speaks both against intolerance and the failure to know God and his commandments.

"**The dew is not dew that has not been petitioned**"—This may allude to the part of the daily *'Amidah* prayer which includes a request for dew or rain according to the season, as well as to the divine flow into the upper and lower worlds in which human beings have an assisting part such as the "**deep confession**" mentioned in the following verse. "Dew" as a symbol for the flow of divine vitality is mentioned also in poems 5 and 37.

"**And still we hear . . .**"—The speaker mocks the various human "solutions" that are cut off from submission to the divine.

## 31

This poem speaks against complacency. Self-confidence and contentment can be dangerous, while being lost brings a person closer to the source of mercy.

"**When the belly is full, and the mind has its sayings, then I fear for my soul**"—In his twenties Cohen experimented with fasting, and his need for self-abnegation would resurface over the years.[67] See also the early poem "It Swings, Jocko," with lines such as: "I want to be hungry, / hungry for food, / for love, for flesh."[68]

---

67. Simmons, *I'm Your Man*, 67–68, 104, 129, 244 etc.
68. Cohen, *The Spice-Box of Earth*, 22.

"**And I am found alone with the husks and the shells**"—In the Lurianic Kabbalah, the "husks" or "shells" (Hebrew *kelipah*, pl. *kelipot*) are the impure material in which the sparks of divine light were entrapped, and represent the forces of evil or the "Other Side" (*Sitra Achara*), the opposite of holiness (see poem 5).

"**Overthrow this even terror with a sweet remembrance: when I was with you, when my soul delighted you, when I was what you wanted**"—This may allude to biblical passages in which the relations between the people of Israel and their Lord were likened to a perfect marital relationship—before turning sour, as the prophets liked to emphasize—for example, Jer 2:2: "Go, and cry in the ears of Jerusalem, saying: Thus saith the Lord: I remember for thee the affection of thy youth, The love of thine espousals; How thou wentest after Me in the wilderness, In a land that was not sown."

"**See how the night has no terror for one who remembers the Name**"—In the background here could be Ps 91, in particular verses 2 and 5: "I will say of the Lord, who is my refuge and my fortress, my God, in whom I trust . . . You shall not be afraid of the terror by night, nor of the arrow that flies by day." It should be pointed out again that in most English translations of the Bible, "the Lord" is the substitute for God's name YHWH ("Jehovah"), which Jews pronounce *ha-Shem* ("the Name," capitalized in this case). On the terror of the dark night see also poem 4.

## 32

This is another "dark" poem in the vein of poem 30, this time round with the motifs of death, old age and failure. Standing out here is the use of the first-person plural, which in the book usually refers to the Jews as a group (see poems 13, 15, 17, 18, 25, and 38). Still, there is a way out of despair by remembering "you."

"**. . . and the good land was taken from us**"—This alludes to warning against the breaking of the Covenant in Deut 11:17, which is recited in the daily prayers: ". . .and ye perish quickly from off the good land which the Lord giveth you."

## II

**"We remember the containing word, the holy channels of commandment, and goodness waiting forever on the Path"**—The use of "commandment" suggests a Jewish context, and allusion is made to the path (or "way") of the Torah or of the Lord, in verses such as Ps 119:33: "Teach me, O Lord, the way of Thy statutes; And I will keep it at every step." There may also be here an echo of Ps 23:6: "Surely goodness and mercy shall follow me all the days of my life; And I shall dwell in the house of the Lord forever." However, the capitalized "Path" may also signify *Dao*, the Way, as it is understood in East Asian cultures, including Zen Buddhism.

**". . . the seventy tongues"**—The source for the notion that the earth is populated by seventy nations speaking seventy tongues is in the "list of nations" in Gen 10, which specifies the seventy decedents of Noah (in the Septuagint there are seventy two names; according to Luke 10, Jesus sent either seventy or seventy two disciples to spread his teaching). This was further elaborated upon in the Talmud and Midrash.

**". . . the hundred darknesses"**—"Darkness" appears nearly twenty times in the book, more often in its second half, including four times in poem 46, and here it appears in an unusual plural form. It sometimes appears as the opposite of light, but in some cases it denotes anxiety and fear. "Light" appears a little more often, twenty three times, evenly distributed between the two parts. Incidentally or not, the poet Paul Celan, known for his post-Holocaust poetry, said in a speech in Germany in 1958: "Only one thing remained reachable, close and secure amid all losses: language. Yes, language. In spite of everything, it remained secure against loss. But it had to go through its own lack of answers, through terrifying silence, through *the thousand darknesses* of murderous speech. It went through. It gave me no words for what was happening, but went through it. Went through it and could resurface, 'enriched' by it all"[69] (italics added). Although it has not been established that Cohen knew Celan's speech, the sentiment is mutual to both poets. Also, the poet Rumi, whose work was well-known to Cohen, has

---

69. Celan, *Collected Prose*, p.34.

the line: "There are a hundred thousand darknesses in thine eye (which arise) from thy wrath against the servants of God".[70]

"**... men of courage strengthening themselves to kindle the light of repentance**"—This verse somewhat resembles the lines from the song "The Old Revolution" on Cohen's second album: "all the brave young men / they're waiting now to see a signal / which some killer will be lighting for pay." From a different direction, "lights of repentance" is the translation of the title of the Hebrew book *Orot Ha-Teshuva* by Rabbi Abraham Isaac Kook, published in 1925. Translated into English in 1968, it may have been familiar to Cohen. Among other things, the book elaborates on the suffering of the soul as it is seeking repentance but offers light gained by the process.

## 33

This poem expresses shame over the speaker's past failures combined with anxiety over the future of his son; the son, as well as the daughter, were mentioned earlier (see poems 10 and 25), but here the focus is on the son.

"**... those who want him with no soul, who have their channels in the bedrooms of the rich and poor**"—A somewhat different version of this line appeared a few years later in "The Tower of Song" on the *I'm Your Man* album (1988): "The rich have got their channels in the bedrooms of the poor."

"**Let him see me coming back**"—The *VP* album includes the song "Coming Back to You" which seems to be addressing a woman and describing the speaker's complicated relations with her but as with many other Cohen songs, an alternative reading is also possible. Lines like "I lived alone but I was only / Coming back to you" express also the spirit of *Book of Mercy* and the speaker's efforts to return to an intimate relationship with the divine. Another song on the *VP* album, "Hunter's Lullaby," expresses a father's anxiety as does the current poem. The song includes lines such as:

---

70. Rumi, *Mathnawí*, Chapter 4, line 3448.

11

> Your father's gone a-hunting
> He's deep in the forest so wild
> And he cannot take his wife with him
> He cannot take his child . . .
>
> Your father's gone a-hunting
> For the beast he'll never bind
> And he leaves a baby sleeping
> And his blessings all behind
>
> Your father's gone a-hunting
> And he's lost his lucky charm
> And he's lost the guardian heart
> That keeps the hunter from the harm

The song expresses the guilt felt by the man who has the endless need to go "hunting"—for women, for pleasure, and even for spiritual peace of mind, artistic inspiration, and solitude—although being aware that he'll never be able to find his true satisfaction, and meanwhile leaves behind children who need him and to whom he may not be able to return. In Cohen's case, in spite of his fears and due to his efforts, he was able to maintain a good and close relationship with his children over the years although his fears must have been acute.[71]

## 34

After the darkness of several consecutive poems and the anxiety expressed in the previous one, the current poem initiates a series of steps through which the speaker regains the feeling of closeness. Although he feels more secure, pain and suffering will resurface again, albeit in a somewhat more subdued expression.

**"You are with me still"**—Here and elsewhere in the book the background may also reflect Ps 23:4: "Yea, though I walk through the valley of the shadow of death, I will fear no evil, for You are

---

71. Simmons, *I'm Your Man*, 310.

with me." The line is repeated at the beginning and the ending of the poem as a sign of reassurance.

**"Even though I have been removed, and my place does not recognize me"**—Once again, Ps 103 is the source of inspiration here (see poem 29), in particular verses 15–16: "As for man, his days are as grass; as a flower of the field, so he flourishes; For the wind passes over it, and it is gone; and the place thereof knows it no more." Similarly, Job 7:1–2 and 9–10: "Is there not a time of service to man upon earth? And are not his days like the days of a hireling? As a servant that eagerly longs for the shadow, and as a hireling that looks for his wages . . . As the cloud is consumed and vanishes away, so he that goes down to the grave shall come up no more. He shall return no more to his house, neither shall his place know him any more." It seems that Cohen could have been familiar with the original Hebrew: although most English translations of these verses use the verb "know" here, he uses "recognize" which is a most appropriate equivalent. Cohen also turned the phrase from the third-person (*lo yakirenu 'od mekomo*) to the first-person. For "place" see also the notes for poem 8.

**"And my beloved says, *I will wait a little while behind this curtain*"**—Once again, the Torah is being personified according to the *Zohar* passage quoted in the notes for poem 3 (and see also poems 12 and 14). It may also refer to God himself, who goes on to say **"– *no, I have waited too long*,"** to which the speaker retorts once again: **"You are with me still."** As in other cases, the image may have a double meaning referring to a terrestrial lover as well.

**"Though I scorched away the tears of return in the forced light of victory"**—The motif of "return" is picked up again following poem 29 (**"gates of return"**) and 32 (**"we cry out to you to return our soul"** and **"lights of repentance"**). The noun **"victory"** is repeated once again in poem 50, but there too not as a true one but as a futile victory. This is also reminiscent of one of the versions of the song "Hallelujah" with the lines: "Yea, I've seen your flag on the marble arch / but love is not some kind of victory march / it's a cold and a very broken Hallelujah."

## II

"**. . . your rebuke still comforts me**"—This could reflect the second half of Ps 23:4 (see above): "Your rod and Your staff, they comfort me." In both cases Cohen added "still," perhaps reflecting on past experiences, especially as a child, when he felt more secure.

"*fix this exile towards my return*"—Here "exile" signifies the condition of the speaker, see notes for poem 24.

"**Though I am unwept, it is your judgment parches me**"—Although the first meaning of "unwept" is passive (similar to "unmourned" or "unsung"), here the speaker seems to use it in an active sense meaning that he cannot cry, following the earlier line: "**I scorched away the tears of return.**" "Judgment" can also refer to the fifth *sefirah* (*Gevurah*), situated on the left side and expressing severity, as the opposite of *Chesed* ("Grace," "Benevolence" or "Love," see poem 29) on the right side. *Tif'eret* ("Mercy"), in the middle, moderates between the two (and see also poem 40).

"**Though I add membrane to membrane against your light**"—Previously the speaker mentioned various kinds of obstacles standing between himself and the light or the Torah, including curtain, veil, wall, and fence, here adding another one which could be more transparent, but he piles up membrane upon membrane still blocking direct contact.

"**. . . when the sun and the moon are shining in the other pan**"—On the sun and moon as symbols of the *sefirot* "Mercy" and "Kingdom" see the notes for poem 13 (although here they seem more prosaic, like eggs frying in a pan).

"**O slow to anger**"—Returning once again to Ps 103, this time verse 8: "The Lord is full of compassion and gracious, slow to anger, and plenteous in mercy." Another example is in Ps 86:15: "But You, O Lord, are a God full of compassion and gracious, slow to anger, and plenteous in mercy and truth." Other verses that include this image are in Exod 34:6-7, which are verses central to the prayers of the *Selichot*, the penitential hymns and prayers recited in the period before and during the Jewish High Holidays (see under poem 1). The speaker here, therefore, is surrounded by the atmosphere of repentance associated with the High Holidays and feeling close to Mercy.

## 35

Like other poems in the book and Cohen's work generally, this poem combines the struggles of faith with erotic expressions (see poem 29). The speaker mentions a list of false starts: he failed because he refused to give in completely.

"**I turned you into a tradition. The tradition devoured its children**"—In the early poems the speaker seeks refuge in the tradition and glorifies it, but he also warns against the danger of it becoming fossilized and losing its living spirit; see under poem 17.

"**I turned you to loneliness**"—See poem 9.

"**If it be your will**"—See the notes for poem 4 and the song of similar title quoted there.

"**... your Bride**"—A symbol of the tenth *sefira*, *Malchut*; see poem 24.

"**This is my offering of incense**"—One of the daily duties of the priests in the Jerusalem temple was to offer incense on a golden altar, morning and evening. It was replaced in Jewish tradition with the reciting of the process of preparing the incense (*Pittum ha-Ketoret*), as described in the Talmud, during the daily morning and afternoon prayers. The use of incense is also common in Catholicism and Buddhism and Cohen used it regularly at home.

"**Bind me to your will**"—For the "will" see poem 4, and for binding poem 10.

## 36

This poem opens with a statement of disbelief. Nevertheless, the speaker is trying to overcome his doubts and turn to the source of mercy. He studies the alternative, the world in which the divine is not present, but this leads to a dead end so once again he seeks another way although it might be painful.

"**Though I don't believe, I come to you now, and I lift my doubt to your mercy**"—Although he does not find in himself the power to truly believe, the speaker does not give up on finding mercy. Cohen expressed a similar position on other occasions such as the verse he added in 1979 to the song "Lover, Lover, Lover" from his album *New Skin for the Old Ceremony* (1974):

> You may come to me in happiness
> Or you may come to me in grief
> You may come to me in deepest faith
> Or you may come in disbelief

**"I made a crown for myself with your blessings"**—See poem 5. The crown appears also in various songs by Cohen such as in "Boogie Street" on the *Ten New Songs* album (quoted in the notes for poem 10), and in "Here It Is" on the same album, with the lines: "Here is your crown, / And your seal and rings; / And here is your love / For all things."

**"The Accuser"**—This is one of the common English renditions for the Hebrew *Satan*, because of his role of accusing people before God (see Job 1). The speaker, describing his own experience, finds that the Accuser **"has no song, and he has no tears"** both of which the speaker is in need of, therefore must turn to the other path (see also poem 42).

**"Give this ghost the form of tears"**—The speaker likened himself to a ghost before in poem 7, where he asked that the ghost be given a stone. For the need for tears see poem 12.

**"Behold him in your court"**—For "court" see also poems 1, 2, and 48.

**". . . the throne of praises"**—In poem 6 the speaker mentioned his "rude chair of praises." "Throne" appears in poems 1, 5, 14, 29, and 46, while "chair" is mentioned in poems 6 and 26 (also "chairs" in poem 11). "Chair" and "throne" can be distinct, but also interchangeable.

## 37

Somewhat similarly to the previous poem, the speaker begins from a place of doubt but then makes progress towards his goal. Many key words appear together in this short poem including "shield" and "name," "mercy" and "law," "dew" and "light," "will" and "love."

"**. . . the will that is bent toward it**"—See poem 4.

"**O name of love**"—See poem 29.

"**. . . the man whom you have cut in half to know you**"—This brings to mind Plato's *Symposium*, in which Aristophanes explains human desire to find the true partner through the myth that in primal times humans had a double body, back to back, and since being separated by Zeus each half is searching for its other half. Eros then is the longing for a lost completeness. A similar idea appears in the Midrash (Bereshit Rabbah 8:1): "In the hour when the Holy One created the first human, He created him [as] an androgyne, 'male and female He created them'. He created [for] him a double-face and sawed him and made him backs, a back here and a back there . . ."." The same tradition is continued in the *Zohar*. For example, the first three *sefirot* are likened to the three Hebrew letters that form the name "Adam" (I, 34b):

> . . . When the three letters had come down below, there was perceived in their form, complete, the name Adam, to comprehend male and female. The female was fastened to the side of the male, and God cast the male into a deep slumber, and . . . then cut the female from him and decked her as a bride and led her to him . . . In the ancient books, I have seen it said that here the word 'one' means 'one woman', that is, the original Lilith, who lay with him and from him conceived. But up to that time, she was no help to him . . .[72]

Following the failure with Lilith, Eve was created as the true "help" (see the notes for poems 4 and 16).

## 38

This is one of a few prose-poems in the book that are read just like regular poems, and in this case can be arranged into four stanzas of three lines each, when considered thematically. Alternatively, according to accents, it could be arranged in five three-line stanzas,

---

72. Scholem, *Zohar, the Book of Splendor*, 31–32.

# II

or five couplets. The speaker here expresses clearly his attachment to Jewish history and his commitment to the tradition.

**"Not far from here, where Rashi taught"**—Rashi is the acronym of Rabbi Shlomo Yitzhaki (1040–1105), who is considered the greatest traditional interpreter of both the Torah and Talmud. Cohen wrote part of his book in Provence, southern France, whereas in fact Rashi was from Troyes and was active in Lorraine, a considerable distance to the north, although in Provence too there were important Jewish communities at the time including those of the early Kabbalists. Cohen may have playfully mentioned Rashi because of the resemblance to Roshi.

**"Beside the church where we were struck to prove some point on Christmas Eve"**—This refers to the Crusades in the Middle Ages when Jews were massacred in Europe and the theological debates in which they were forced to participate. Cohen's historical awareness ever since his earliest writing is demonstrated in poems such as "For Wilf and His House" in his very first poetry collection.[73] For Cohen's ambivalent feelings towards France see the ironical passage "Why I Love France."[74]

**". . . with broken heart and joyous word"**—As in the song "Hallelujah" (see under poems 4 and 7), "broken" and "joyous" are not exclusive but complimentary. Cohen must have been aware of the saying attributed to the Hasidic Rabbi Menachem Mendel of Kotzk: "There is nothing as whole as a broken heart" (see more about him under poems 39 and 40). The notion of worshiping God with joy including by singing and dancing is central to the teaching of Hasidism, and its influence on Cohen stands out in the following poems.

**"To have this work, to fill this line"**—This is a relatively rare case in this book in which the speaker mentions his work in positive terms.

---

73. Cohen, *Let Us Compare Mythologies*, 16–17. The poem contains the line which serves as the title of the book; see also Scobie, *Leonard Cohen*, 22–23; Simmons, *I'm Your Man*, 48.

74. Cohen, *Book of Longing*, 115.

**"to be so blessed for my mother's sake, for my father's wine"**—The father and mother were mentioned together once before in poem 5 (see the notes there, and also the notes for poems 9 and 24). In Jewish tradition, the father reads a blessing (*Kiddush*) over a cup of wine before the meal on the Sabbath eve and on certain holidays.

## 39

This poem can be read as a prayer before sleeping. In the traditional Jewish prayer (see below) the enemy is death, and this may be the intention here too. The poem contrasts solitude, failure and loss on the one hand with unity, mercy and light on the other, but the speaker cannot be in touch with the latter before going through the former.

In this and a few other poems the language of the traditional prayer before retiring at night can be detected. Following are a few relevant verses out of this quite long prayer (*Kri'at Shem'a 'al hamitah*), appearing in slightly different versions in every Jewish *Siddur*:

> May it be your will, Lord my God and God of my fathers, that I shall sin no more. The sins that I have committed, erase in Your abounding mercies, but not through suffering or severe illnesses . . . Blessed are You, Lord our God, King of the universe, who causes the bonds of sleep to fall upon my eyes and slumber upon my eyelids, and who gives light to the apple of the eye . . . Do not bring us into sin, nor into temptation or scorn. May the good inclination master over me and the bad inclination not master over me. Let my thoughts not trouble me, nor bad dreams, nor sinful fancies, and may my bed be perfect before You. Give light to my eyes lest I sleep the sleep of death. Blessed are You, Lord, who in His glory gives light to the whole world.

**"All that is not you"**—This may be related to the verse in Isa 6:3: "the whole earth is full of His glory," as well as to the saying from the *Zohar* (Tikkunei Zohar 57): "There is no place vacant of him in the higher or the lower [worlds]," which is particularly popular in Hasidic writings. The Hasidic world-view is based on the notion designated by scholars with the term *panentheism*, the belief that the divine is present in each aspect of the universe, but is also greater than it (as distinguished from *pantheism*, the worldview associated with Spinoza, according to which the divine and the universe are identical): "God is *in* everything" rather than "all is God." According to this notion, prevalent in this book and in the rest of Cohen's work, one does not have to detach oneself from the mundane reality in order to seek the divine in a transcendent one. Rather, one can discover the immanence of a transcended reality in the here and now (see also the notes for poems 8 and 43). Cohen revealed in interviews that he conversed with "Hasidic sages," probably mostly of the *Chabad* movement, who may have familiarized him with this and other notions.

**"It is you I welcome here"**—Also relevant in this context is the saying attributed to Rabbi Menachem Mendel of Kotzk, the Hasidic rabbi who lived in eastern Poland and died in 1859: "Where does God reside? Wherever He is welcome." Another common translation is: "Where is God to be found? In the place where He is given entry." There are several points of contact between the world of Cohen and that of the rabbi of Kotzk, including the fact that both had suffered from depression—the rabbi remained secluded in his room for years, his followers unable to see his face—and their independent and defiant habits of thought. Unlike other Hasidic rabbis, the rabbi of Kotzk emphasized the conflicts inherent in human life, rather than the joys, and demanded that his followers act in extreme ways, that might expose them to accusations and ridicule. Another saying attributed to him that could have impressed Cohen is: "Only horses walk in the middle of the road; man should walk on the edges." Following the Midrashic dictum concerning the life-stages of man, according to which "at old age he is like a monkey" (Qohelet Rabbah 1:2), the rabbi's rejoinder was: "He imitates himself" (see also the notes for poems 38, 40, and 41).

Another Hasidic notion that may be relevant to the current cluster of poems is *devekut* ("dedication," more literally "clinging on" to God). While earlier in Judaism this was an ideal reserved for persons of unique religious level, in Hasidism *devekut* was considered attainable by any person whose mind always concentrate on God. One technique for achieving this was through meditating on the four letters of the Name (YHWH) (see also poem 48).

## 40

While the previous poem can be read as a prayer before sleep, the current one could be a prayer on awakening. The speaker prays to be able to overcome his doubts and weaknesses and reconnect with the will of the divine.

"**. . . let the puppet fall among the strings**"—Although "marionette" could have been expected here, "puppet" is used. See also Cohen's poem "Puppets,"[75] which describes a world devoid of will. Here he speaks about giving up his own "tiny will" in order to submit to the "authentic will" of mercy (see under poem 4).

"**Let me raise your kingdom to the beauty of your name**"—In the Kabbalah, each *sefira* is identified with, among other symbols, one of God's biblical names. *Tif'eret* ("Mercy") is, for example, identified with the Name (YHWH); it is also translated sometimes as "beauty." The unification of the male and female aspects *Tif'eret* and *Malchut*, which the Kabbalists strive to assist, is possibly hinted at here. In a passage in *Book of Longing* quoted twice before,[76] the speaker likens himself to the High Priest who enters the Holy of Holies, the innermost part of the Jerusalem temple, on the Day of Atonement, saying: "I will enter the chamber of the Bride and the Bridegroom, and no one will follow me."

"**. . . the heart that is not broken enough**"—Once again, following the previous two poems, this may refer to the saying by Rabbi Menachem Mendel of Kotzk: "There is nothing as whole as

---

75. Cohen, *Book of Longing*, 160, and recited on the album *Thanks for the Dance*.

76. Cohen, *Book of Longing*, 34.

a broken heart," meaning that a person must approach the divine out of brokenness and even hopelessness, seeking to be accepted. And as the speaker here puts it: **"Then the surface of the world is restored, then he can walk and build a will."** In this context, it is useful to consider the following relatively long quotation from the *Zohar*. Its contents overlap with many of the themes and images that come up throughout *Book of Mercy*, including the relatively rare mention of joy (poem 19) and offering (poem 35), as well as the image of the crown, references to Torah, sin, penitence, the priests' cultic labor, singing—and specifically the Torah singing (see poem 5, although in this text it may refer simply to the chanting of the Torah in the synagogue)—and more (III, 8ab):

> Discoursing on the text: "Serve the Lord with joy, come before his presence with singing" [Ps 100:2], Rabbi Judah said: We have learned that the service of God which is not made with joy and zeal, that service is imperfect. But what if a man sins against the commands of the law, and then in repentance goes to offer service to God? Of what countenance can a man be on such occasion standing before the Lord? Verily, he is then grieved of heart and penitent of spirit, and how then shall he show joy and singing? The truth is, however, that the priests and Levites did it on his behalf; it was the priest who performed the rejoicing, because he is far from chastisement, and is bound ever to manifest a joyful countenance, more so than the others. Furthermore, his crown is decisive. And as for the singing, this the Levites performed, whose function it was. Thus, the priest was stationed by the man and with fitting words he unified the holy Name in joy, and at the same time the Levites performed the singing . . . Now that offerings no longer exist, one who sins before his Lord and then returns to Him, surely with a bitter soul, with sorrow, weeping and a broken spirit, how can he show joy and singing which he is lacking? The answer is that praises offered to his Lord, joy of the Torah and singing of the Torah, these are the joy and the singing.[77]

---

77. Scholem, *Zohar, the Book of Splendor*, 112–13, adding a few lines which were omitted in this translation.

"**Let us not be tested**"—From the traditional Morning Blessings (*Birchot ha-Shachar*): "And may it be Your will, Lord our God and God of our fathers, to accustom us to the study of Your Torah, and to make us cleave to Your commandments. Do not bring us into sin, nor into transgression or iniquity, not into temptation [= test, *nisayon*] or scorn; and may the evil inclination not have master over us."

"**Blessed are you who creates and destroys, who sits in judgment on numberless worlds**"—See the notes for poem 24. "Blessed" appears in the book more frequently than any other adjective: twenty times in five poems of part I, and twenty two times in eleven poems of part II, including in every poem from 40 to 50 except for 43. This is a reflection of the more conciliatory and prayer-like tone of part II and in particular its final poems, as mentioned earlier.


## 41

The feeling of being lost, with which the book opened, has not been resolved yet although the speaker here is in a dialogue with the source of mercy, and the love in his heart is directed towards that source.

"**Heart**," which symbolizes not only love but feelings generally, appears in this poem three times and in the whole book about sixty five times, more than any other noun. It appears also in most songs on the *VP* album, including in the title of the song "Heart with No Companion," the language and spirit of which closely resemble those of *Book of Mercy*, with lines such as:

> I greet you from the other side
> Of sorrow and despair
> With a love so vast and shattered
> It will reach you everywhere . . .
>
> For the heart with no companion
> For the soul without a king
> For the prima ballerina
> Who cannot dance to anything

# II

> Through the days of shame that are coming
> Through the nights of wild distress
> Tho' your promise count for nothing
> You must keep it nonetheless . . .

**"Bind me, ease of my heart, bind me to your love"**—The motif of the binding occurs here once again, as it does earlier and later in the book (see poems 4 and 10 above, 42 and 48 below).

**". . . you hide me in the shelter of your name"**—"Shelter" appeared once before in poem 16: **"the low-built shelter of repentance"** (**"sheltered"** appeared in poem 14), and will appear several more times later on (see poems 44, 46, and 47). It can be an alternative to the more frequent "shield," and may also stem from certain biblical or liturgical verses, such as Ps 91:1–3: "O you who dwell in the shelter of the Most High, and abide in the protection of the Almighty, I say of the Lord, my refuge and my fortress, my God, in whom I trust, that He will deliver you from the snare of the fowler, and from the destructive plague."

**". . . to bless your name in speechlessness"**—Other sayings of the Rabbi of Kotzk (see under poems 39 and 40) are: "There is no louder shout than silence"; "You don't call to the Lord loudly but quietly, from inside the heart."

**"Blessed are you in the smallness of your whispering"**—This may be an allusion to the encounter in the wilderness between the prophet Elijah and the divine in I Kgs 19, the climax of which is the appearance of YHWH in "a still small voice," 19:12. The speaker also wishes to convey the difficulty in hearing the true voice of the divine in our daily life, and the effort required in order to do so.

**"Blessed are you who speaks to the unworthy"**—Apart from the Rabbi of Kotzk, there was another unique Hasidic leader to whom the saying "There is nothing as whole as a broken heart" is sometimes attributed, Rabbi Nachman of Bratslav (1772–1810). He was an exceptionally original thinker and storyteller, and after his death his followers did not appoint a successor, but regard him as their rabbi even to this day. Although he stressed the importance of joy, Rabbi Nachman was aware of the obstacles standing between a person burdened by sinfulness and gaining intimacy with the divine. Realizing that the Hasid must pass through melancholy in order to achieve joy, he prescribed the daily practice of *hitbodedut* or "lonely meditation," in which the Hasid would pour out his soul to God in longing and contrition. It is very likely that Cohen was familiar with Rabbi Nachman of Bratslav's teachings and was influenced by them.

## 42

This poem continues the theme of the previous one. Like the following one, it is short and succinct, but contains many charged words, including the frequent "you," "name," "shield," and "mercy," as well as "binding," and several others.

**"It is to you I turn"**—A similar expression is repeated twice again in the following sentences. "Turning" and "returning" are words of repentance (*teshuva* in Hebrew), which the speaker keeps bringing up; see poems 16, 29, 32, and 34.

**"The table stands on tiptoe"**—"Table" is a word with special meaning for Cohen in his life and work. Other such words are "room" and "window," although they do not stand out in *Book of Mercy*: "room" appears in it only three times, while "window" does not appear literally at all, although viewing through it is implied in poem 12. The table can be the one used for writing, to gather the family around, and even as a substitute for the altar (see also poems 13, 18, and 46). Here the table stands on tiptoe, probably in anticipation of reconnecting with the divine, enhancing its role as an altar, also expressing the excitement of the speaker.

**". . . my song in the house of night"**—The expression "the house of night" appears also at the end of poem 14 ("house" is also in poems 4, 23, 24, and 29, "household" in poem 10). For "night" see the notes for poems 4 and 31.

**"The Accuser"**—See poem 36. It is also worthwhile mentioning the Talmudic dictum (b. Bava Batra 16a): "Satan, the evil inclination, and the Angel of Death are all one" (see also the notes for poems 2 and 4).

"... **who unifies the upward heart**"—See also poem 50, and the notes for poem 41.

"... **and binds this song to the rock**"—This verse may allude to both the binding of Isaac and to Prometheus being chained to the rock. "Rock" itself can allude to "Rock of Ages," which according to the famous hymn refers to Jesus, as well as being the first line in the English translation of the major Hanukah song (*Ma'oz Tzur* in Hebrew). It is also short for "rock and roll," for the Hall of Fame of which Cohen was inducted in 2008, to his considerable surprise.

## 43

In this short poem the word which stands out is "holy," an adjective which appears relatively rarely in the book (see poems 24, 29, and 32). The poem echoes the "Holiness verse" (Isa 6:3, see the notes to poem 1), with the anaphoric repetition of "Holy."

"**Holy are the hands that are raised to you**"—On the raising of the hands see in the notes for poem 30.

"**Holy is the fire between your will and ours**"—On the two wills see the notes for poem 4.

"**Holy is that which is unredeemed**"—The entire reality contains holiness. According to the Lurianic Kabbalah, the sparks of holiness are scattered everywhere awaiting being drawn back to their source through human beings' prayers and other efforts. This idea has an important place in Hasidism expressed through the notion of "worship through corporeality" (*'avodah be-gashmi'yut*). As mentioned earlier (see the notes for poem 39), Hasidism emphasized the notion of divine immanence in the whole of reality which lifted the value of mundane secular activities to that of religious rituals. The line separating the sacred and the profane became blurred.

"**Holy, and shining with a great light, is every living thing**"—This too is in accordance with the "panentheistic" world view of Hasidism.

"**. . . until your name is praised forever**"—Another allusion to the *Kaddish* (see poem 9). Cohen returned to the *Kaddish* once again in the refrain of the eponymous song on his final album, *You Want It Darker*, with a direct quote of the first words of the prayer: "Magnified and sanctified / Be Thy Holy Name."

## 44

The speaker expresses his inadequacy compared with the sages of esotericism and the Kabbalah, and perhaps also of Zen but he finds simpler ways to turn and ask for mercy in everyday reality. This poem expresses clearly the speaker's abstinence from attempting mystical ascending which is beyond his abilities or wishes.

"**The meditations of the great**"—This may include the sages of various faiths who tried to reach the highest heavens through numerous methods of meditation.

"**. . . the entwining of the letters**"—Refers to the Midrashic and Kabbalistic practices which uncover hidden meanings in the letters of the Torah.

"**I cannot climb down to the vehicles of holiness**"—This refers to the early Jewish sages of esoteric wisdom in the first centuries CE who are sometimes known by the elliptical term "descenders of the chariot" (*yordei ha-merkavah*) although they were supposed to ascend in it rather than descend into that vehicle. The "chariot" is based on the vision in Ezek 1 (and probably also on Elijah's chariot in 2 Kgs 2:11–12). The literature developed around it is known as "Merkavah mysticism," part of the larger corpus of the "Books of the Palaces and the Chariot" (see also notes for poem 1). This literature had wide-spread influence before the emergence of the Kabbalah proper in the twelfth century CE.

"**. . . and my dreams do not ascend**"—In many cultures dreams are considered a common way of receiving messages from a divine source. In Jewish tradition this is evident throughout the Bible, and in later stages in books such as the thirteenth century *Responsa from Heaven* in which legal matters were solved based on "dream questions," or the early seventeenth century *The Book* *of Visions* by Rabbi Haim Vital, a leading exponent of the Lurianic Kabbalah, reporting his and others' messianic dreams.

"**. . . with broom and rag**"—A metaphor for the simpler means for those who cannot do as the sages did. This may also reflect life in a Zen monastery where the novices clean the place each day, sometimes while running, in order to burn off some of the energy accumulated during meditation.

"**. . . my portion**"—In Jewish tradition "portion" refers to the place each person will have in the world to come. According to the chapter dedicated to this subject in the Mishna and Talmud (Perek Chelek, tractate Sanhedrin), each and every person has a portion reserved specifically for themselves, but which they might lose through religious transgressions. The origin of the idea may be Lam 3:24: "The Lord is my portion, says my soul, therefore will I hope in Him."

## 45

This prose-poem (like poem 38) gives itself over to being arranged in the form of poetry, in this case five units of four, three, four, four, and five lines thematically and anaphorically although other prosodic considerations may be applied. The use of anaphora, the almost hypnotic repetition of the same words at the beginning of every line in each unit (except for the middle one), stands out. The repetitive style is also reminiscent of Sufi poetry with which Cohen was familiar,[78] and there are also various models in English poetry and the Psalms.

"**I go through a pinhole of light**"—See the following poem, 46.

"**Blessed are you who brings chains out of the darkness**"— Ironically, the language of this verse seems to follow the traditional Jewish blessing over bread: "Blessed are You, Lord our God, King of the Universe, who brings forth bread from the earth." The divine presence in the world also serves to reveal evil, including

---

78. See my article "Speaking Sweetly from 'The Window': Reading Leonard Cohen's Song."

oppression symbolized by chains, exposing it out of its darkness, thus making it possible to protest against it.

Ever since the mid 1980's Cohen would occasionally sing in live performances a song titled "Born in Chains," which was reintroduced during his 2010 tour and was finally released on his 2014 album *Popular Problems*. The song was presumably written during the same period as the current book and the *VP* album, an album that had but nine songs, and it might have been expected that this song be included but Cohen felt it was unfinished and kept writing different versions of it. Cohen said in an interview back in 1988:

> ... that song started off as a song about the exodus of the Hebrew people from Egypt. As a metaphor for the journey of the soul from bondage into freedom. It started out, I was born in chains but I was taken out of Egypt / I was bound to a burden but the burden it was raised / Lord I can no longer keep this secret / Blessed is the name, the name be praised. It went on like that for a long, long time, and I went into the studio and tried to sing this song about how "I was born in chains and I was taken . . ." But I wasn't born in chains and I wasn't taken out of Egypt, and not only that, but I was on the edge of what was going to become a very serious nervous breakdown. So I hadn't had the burden lifted and the whole thing was a lie! It was wishful thinking. And this song, "Taken Out of Egypt," took months and months to write. Nobody believes me when I say these things but I have the notebooks and I don't fill them in an evening. And there were many of them. So it wasn't as if I had an endless supply of songs: I had to start over. And I was saying to myself, "What is my life?" and that's when I started writing that lyric: I stumble out of bed / I got ready for the struggle / I smoked a cigarette / And I tightened up my gut / I said this can't be me / Must be my double / And I can't forget / I can't forget / But I don't remember what. That was really true.[79]

In *Book of Mercy* "chain" occurs in poem 33, and "chained" in poem 4. There seems to be a distinction in Cohen's mind between

---

79. Rowland, "Leonard Cohen's Nervous Breakthrough."

being "bound" as a positive experience, and "chained" as a negative one. "Chains" also reappears in a later song, "Show Me the Place" on the *Old Ideas* album:

> The troubles came
> I saved what I could save
> A thread of light
> A particle a wave
> But there were chains
> So I hastened to behave
> There were chains
> So I loved you like a slave

**"Blessed are you, whose name is in the world"**—Once again, the existence of the divine presence represented by the name in this world is important for the speaker rather than seeking it in other worlds.

## 46

A prayer for help in which the name is discovered out of pain. This poem also expresses the messianic hope for a new creation. The speaker's mental state and the world state reflect each other.

"**. . . help me at my aimless table**"—On the table see poem 42; there the table was expressing excitement, while here it is defined as "aimless," as an expression of the speaker's helplessness (see also poems 13 and 18).

"**Blessed are you who speaks from the darkness**"—Years later Cohen would write the song "Darkness," released on the *Old Ideas* album. "Blessed are you" is a shortened version of the common "Blessed are You, Lord our God, King of the Universe." It is perhaps shortened in order not to create too distinct a similarity with the *Siddur*, or to avoid blasphemy.

"**The ruins signal your power**"—"Power" can signify the fifth *sefirah* (*Gevurah*), also known as "Justice" (see poem 34).

"**. . . and all things crack that your throne be restored to the heart**"—Some years later Cohen would write the song "Anthem," released on *The Future* album, including the lines that became one of his most famous quotes: "There is a crack in everything / That's how the light gets in." This image goes back to the Kabbalistic notion of the breaking of the vessels and the spreading of the sparks (Cohen confirmed in his interview with Kurzweil that these lines contain "a Jewish idea"); see also the previous poem. The restoration of the throne is an image which appears in the book right from the first poem.

"**Let each man be sheltered in the fortress of your name . . . the towers of your law**"—The speaker wishes to return to the essentials, the "name" and the "law" which are like fortresses and towers, stable and constant and giving refuge to each person individually serving also as the base for the community (see also the following poem).

"**Create the world again**"—See poem 24.

"**. . . on the foundation of your light**"—See poem 8.

## 47

The speaker admits his failure in rescuing his soul by himself, and turns once again to the source of mercy, feeling secure. Here too the three key words "shield," "name," and "mercy" appear together (as in poems 9, 37, and 42).

"**I struggled with shapes and with numbers**"—Among other things, this could allude to the *I Ching* or *Classic of Changes*, the Chinese book in which line hexagrams are used for divination. Cohen is known to have studied it closely especially during his twenties.[80]

"**. . . a shelter for my soul**"—See poem 41.

"**. . . solitude to solitude all your creatures speak**"—Even when feeling closer to the source of mercy or to other human beings, the experience of solitude or loneliness remains a fundamental one. In the song "Waiting for the Miracle" on the album *The Future*, Cohen proposes to his companion, but still does not regard marriage as a remedy for loneliness: "Ah baby, let's get married,

---

80. Simmons, *I'm Your Man*, 82, etc.

/ we've been alone too long. / Let's be alone together. / Let's see if we're that strong" (in reality Cohen continued to wait for the miracle, and rather than getting married he retired to the Zen monastery for five years).

## 48

This poem brings together many of the motifs that appear throughout the book—including sin, the name, the king, the court, the *sefirot*, the will, the heart, mercy, breathing, binding, solitude, and more—while giving them new expressions. As in some earlier cases in the book, as well as in the song "Hallelujah," the speaker assumes the persona of the old king, the poet of the Psalms, who realizes his failure to create a reality to meet his expectations, and as in the previous poem his only refuge is asking for mercy.

"**I established a court, and I fell asleep under a crown**"—See poems 1, 2, and 5; the final poems close a circle with the first ones.

"**. . . and I dreamed I could rule the wicked**"—"Wicked" or "base" people appear several times in King David's life story (for example, 1 Sam 25:17, 30:22; 2 Sam 20:1). He had complicated relations with his sister's belligerent sons, as he complains in 2 Sam 3:39: "And I am this day weak, and just anointed king; and these men the sons of Zeruiah are too hard for me; the Lord reward the evildoer according to his wickedness." It is also an image for the speaker's failure to control the evil inclination and other drives, and perhaps also refers to human beings' hubris in believing they can rule the world.

"**. . . the breath which you breathe into me**"—See poems 7 and 28.

"**. . . wisdom . . . understanding**"—Together with "crown" as in some other cases such as poem 5, the three highest *sefirot* are alluded to here.

"**Blessed is the name of the glory of your kingdom forever and ever**"—Another variation on the *Shema* (see poem 6): here it is "your kingdom" instead of "his kingdom" as in the prayer.

"... **the one who keeps faith with those who sleep in the dust**"—Quoting once again directly from the *Siddur*, this time from the daily *'Amidah* prayer (as in poems 7, 8, 20, and 30).

"**Bind me, intimate, bind me to your wakefulness**"—The verb "bind" which is often repeated in the book (see in particular poems 10, 35, and 41), is repeated twice in the final verse of this poem as an expression of the effort and hope of establishing a permanent connection, even an intimate one, with the divine, and perhaps also has to do with the Hasidic notion of *devekut* (see the notes for poem 39). It is possible that with "intimate" Cohen alludes to the first words of the popular Kabbalistic hymn by the sixteenth century Rabbi Elazar Azikri, *Yedid Nefesh*, more commonly translated "Beloved of the soul."

## 49

This poem continues in the same vein as the two previous ones admitting to helplessness and seeking support. The motif of brokenness stands out here.

"**All my life is broken unto you**"—See poems 4 and 10, among others.

"**Lift me up to the wrestling of faith**"—Alluding once again to the story of Jacob in Genesis 32; see poems 10 and 27.

"**... where the sparks go out**"—The fallen sparks of the divine light; see poems 1, 43, and 46.

"**Face me to the rays of love, O source of light, or face me to the majesty of your darkness**"—On the combination of light and darkness see the notes for poem 10. Reality is broken in half but light and darkness are complementary opposites (also in the spirit of Daoism expressed in the principle of "yin and yang"). Also, in John Milton's *Paradise Lost*, Mammon, one of the fallen angels describes God the Father as sometimes appearing in darkness which obscures his throne: "And with the Majesty of darkness round /

Covers his Throne; from whence deep thunders roar".[81] For the speaker here "darkness" must refer to God's hidden face.

"**. . . do not leave me here, where death is forgotten, and the new thing grins**"—Forgetting death must lead to a life of illusion. The speaker views the future with alarm. In the song "Coming Back to You" on the *VP* album Cohen says:

> And springtime starts but then it stops
> In the name of something new
> And all the senses rise against this
> Coming back to you.

In the song "The Future" Cohen foresees a future no less terrible than the past: "I've seen the future, brother: it is murder."

## 50

The final poem is very short, similar in length to poems 3 and 9 and even a little shorter, expressing confidence in the possibility of finding a way back in spite of losing one's way.

"**. . . your name unifies the heart**"—As in the symbol on the book's cover; see also poems 41 and 42.

"Blessed is the one who waits in the traveller's heart for his turning"—The final line is once again in the spirit, if not the exact language, of the *Siddur*. For "turning" see poem 42.

---

81. Keriggan et al., *The Complete Poetry and Essential Prose of John Milton*, 2:266–67, 331. I am grateful to Louis Schwartz for suggesting this quote.

# Conclusion

ON 13 OCTOBER 2016, three and a half weeks prior to his death, Leonard Cohen held his last press conference at the Canadian consulate in Los Angeles. The occasion was the release of his album *You Want It Darker*. When asked about the moment of inspiration for the lyrics "I'm ready, My Lord" in the eponymous song on the album, Cohen said:

> I don't really know the genesis, the origin. That *hineni*, that declaration of readiness no matter what the outcome, that's a part of everyone's soul. We all are motivated by deep impulses and deep appetites to serve even though we may not be able to locate that which we are willing to serve. So this is just a part of my nature and I think everybody else's nature to offer oneself at the moment, at the critical moment when the emergency becomes articulate. It is only when the emergency becomes articulate that we can locate that willingness to serve.[82]

When asked about the importance of religion in his life, Cohen responded:

> I have never thought of myself as a religious person. I don't have any spiritual strategy. I kind of limp along like so many of us do in these realms. Occasionally I've felt the grace of another presence in my life, but I can't build any kind of spiritual structure on that. So I feel this is a

---

82. *Last Press Conference*, transcribed from audio recording.

vocabulary that I grew up with, this biblical landscape is very familiar to me and it's natural that I use those landmarks as references. Once they were universal references and everybody understood and knew them and located them. That's no longer the case today, but it is still my landscape. I try to make those references I try to make sure that they are not too obscure. But outside of that I can't, I dare not claim anything in the spiritual realm for my own.[83]

Some thirty-two years after the publication of *Book of Mercy*, Cohen was still speaking in lines that would sound familiar to readers of the book and that are compatible with things he was saying in interviews at the time of its composition and publication. Although he had no clear "spiritual strategy," he built his work on top of the "biblical landscape." And although he may not have been able to locate that which he was willing to serve, "when the emergency becomes articulate" he was able to find "that willingness to serve." That emergency is articulated in various modes throughout *Book of Mercy*, as it is also articulated in earlier and later poems and songs. Cohen never tried to provide his audience with clear theological guidelines nor with concrete answers to his own queries. Rather, he expressed his bewilderment poetically, pointing to the ways in which he tried to find solace. The very poetic nature of this expression is what makes it so compelling.

Cohen never positioned himself as a guru, always as a disciple or at most a companion. Occasionally he assumed the position of a prophet, admonishing and foreseeing a bleak future, but he was at his best when expressing the struggles of his soul in love, life and faith, frankly but sophisticatedly. These expressions struck a chord in the hearts and minds of those who felt he was articulating their own struggles, but who could not say it as well as he did through word and music. Like any true artist, he channeled the feelings and needs of the many and distilled them in his unique mode of creativity. In some cases these assumed the form of very personal prayers that can still be shared by others, and this is what he offered in *Book of Mercy*.

83. *Last Press Conference*, transcribed from audio recording.

# Bibliography and Discography

## 1. THE WORK OF LEONARD COHEN REFERRED TO OR QUOTED

### Books, in order of publication

Cohen, Leonard. *Let Us Compare Mythologies*. Toronto: McGill Poetry Series 1. New York: HarperCollins, 2007.
———. *The Spice-Box of Earth*. New York: Bantam, 1968.
———. *The Favourite Game*. London: Panther, 1973.
———. *Beautiful Losers*. London: Panther, 1973.
———. *Death of a Lady's Man*. Toronto: McClelland and Stewart, 1978.
———. *Book of Mercy*. Toronto: McClelland and Stewart, 1984.
———. *Stranger Music—Selected Poems and Songs*. Toronto: McClelland and Stewart, 1993.
———. *Book of Longing*. Toronto: McClelland and Stewart, 2006.

### Albums, in order of publication

Cohen, Leonard. *Songs of Leonard Cohen*. Columbia. 1967.
———. *Songs from a Room*. Columbia. 1969.
———. *Songs of Love and Hate*. Columbia. 1971.
———. *Live Songs*. Columbia. 1973.
———. *New Skin for the Old Ceremony*. Columbia. 1974.
———. *Death of a Ladies' Man*. Columbia. 1977.
———. *Recent Songs*. Columbia. 1979.
———. *Various Positions*. Columbia. 1984.
———. *I'm Your Man*. Columbia. 1988.
———. *The Future*. Columbia. 1992.

BIBLIOGRAPHY AND DISCOGRAPHY

———. *Ten New Songs*. Columbia. 2001.
———. *Dear Heather*. Columbia. 2004.
———. *Old Ideas*. Columbia. 2012.
———. *Popular Problems*. Columbia. 2014.
———. *You Want It Darker*. Columbia. 2016.
———. *Thanks for the dance*. Columbia. 2019.

## 2. JEWISH AND OTHER SOURCES

### The Hebrew Bible

English versions of biblical verses quoted in the notes are mostly according to *Tanakh: The Holy Scripture*. The Jewish Publication Society of America 1917 translation, occasionally modified.
[A later version of this translation was published in 1985 and so was not available to Cohen when compiling his book; he may have been influenced by other English Bibles including the King James Version, but he was no doubt familiar with the above Jewish one].

### The Jewish Prayer Book

*Siddur Tehilat Hashem, Nusach Ha-Ari Zal* [. . .]. New York: Merkos L'Inyonei Chinuch, 2013.
[Cohen indicated in interviews that during the period of writing *Book of Mercy* he was using a bilingual prayer book issued by Chabad similar to the one quoted here].

### Mishna, Talmud and Midrash

Quotes are mostly according to the English versions found on the *Sefaria* website.

### Sefer Ha-Zohar

Scholem, Gershom. *Zohar, the Book of Splendor: Basic Readings from the Kabbalah*. New York: Schocken, 1949.
[This book, containing a selection of paragraphs from the *Zohar* in English translation, must have been familiar to Cohen].

BIBLIOGRAPHY AND DISCOGRAPHY

## New Testament:

Quoted from the New International Version.

## 3. INTERVIEWS, BIOGRAPHIES AND STUDIES

### Interviews

Benazon, Michael. "Leonard Cohen of Montreal: Interview." *Matrix* 23 (Fall, 1986) 43–55.
Burger, Jeff, ed. *Leonard Cohen on Leonard Cohen: Interviews and Encounters.* Chicago Review Press, 2014.
Gzowsky, Peter. "Leonard Cohen at 50." Radio interview with Leonard Cohen for CBC (1984). http://www.cbc.ca/archives/categories/arts-entertainment/music/leonard-cohen-canadas-melancholy-bard/cohen-at-50.html.
Kurzweil, Arthur. "I *Am* the Little Jew Who Wrote the Bible: A Conversation Between Leonard Cohen and Arthur Kurzweil." In *Leonard Cohen on Leonard Cohen: Interviews and Encounters*, edited by Jeff Burger, 369–93. Chicago Review Press, 2014.
Rowland, Mark. "Leonard Cohen's Nervous Breakthrough." *Musician*, July 1988. https://www.rocksbackpages.com/Library/Article/leonard-cohens-nervous-breakthrough.
Sward, Robert. "An interview with Leonard Cohen." *The Malahat Review* 77 (1986) 58–59. In *Leonard Cohen on Leonard Cohen: Interviews and Encounters*, edited by Jeff Burger, 163–71. Chicago Review Press, 2014.
Turner, Steve. "Leonard Cohen: The Profits of Doom." *Q* (UK), April 1988. In *Leonard Cohen on Leonard Cohen: Interviews and Encounters*, edited by Jeff Burger, 207–13. Chicago Review Press, 2014.
Twigg, Alan. "Leonard Cohen." In *Strong Voices: Conversations with Fifty Canadian Authors*. Madeira Park, BC: Harbour, 1988.

### Internet Chat (18 October 2001)

Leonard Cohen Internet chat transcript: http://www.canoe.ca/JamChat/leonardcohen.html. Retrieved 22 August, 2011.

### Last press conference (13 October 2016)

At the Canadian Consulate, Los Angeles; full audio on National Public Radio's *All Songs Considered*. https://www.npr.org/sections/allsongs/2016/11/11/501659528/hear-one-of-leonard-cohens-final-interviews

BIBLIOGRAPHY AND DISCOGRAPHY

## Biographies

Nadel, Ira B. *Various Positions: A Life of Leonard Cohen*. Austin: Austin University of Texas Press, 2007.
Simmons, Sylvie. *I'm Your Man: The Life of Leonard Cohen*. London: Vintage, 2017.

## Studies

Cohen, Doron B. "Speaking Sweetly from 'The Window': Reading Leonard Cohen's Song." *Journal of the Interdisciplinary of Monotheistic Religions* 6 (2010) 106–29. https://cismor.jp/uploads-images/sites/3/2014/03/Speaking-Sweety-from-.pdf.
Pally, Marcia, *From This Broken Hill I Sing To You: God, Sex, and Politics in the Work of Leonard Cohen*. London: t&tclarck, 2021.
Scobie, Stephen. *Leonard Cohen*. Studies in Canadian Literature. Vancouver: Douglas & McIntyre, 1978.
Wolfson, Elliot R. "New Jerusalem Glowing: Songs and Poems of Leonard Cohen in a Kabbalistic Key." *Kabbalah: Journal for the Study of Jewish Mystical Texts* 15 (2006) 103–53.

## Other Sources Quoted

Celan, Paul. *Collected Prose*. Translated by Rosmarie Waldrop. Manchester: Carcanet, 1986.
Kerrigan, William, John Rumrich, and Stephen Fallon, eds. *The Complete Poetry and Essential Prose of John Milton*. New York: The Modern Library, 2007.
Pethica, James, ed. *Yeats's Poetry, Drama, and Prose*. New York: Norton, 2000.
Rumi. *The Mathnawí of Jalálu'ddín Rúmí, Edited from the Oldest Manuscripts Available: with Critical Notes, Translation, & Commentary by Reynold A. Nicholson*. (Cambridge, UK: E. J. W. Gibb Memorial Trust, 1926; rpt. 1960, 1968, 1977, 1982, 1990, Vol. IV.
Suzuki, D. T. *Zen Buddhism: Selected Writings of D. T. Suzuki*. Edited by William Barrett. Garden City: Doubleday, 1956.

## Major Websites

The Leonard Cohen Files. Managed by Jarkko Arjatsalo. http://www.leonardcohenfiles.com/.
Speaking Cohen. Managed by Marie Mazur. http://www.speakingcohen.com/.
Chords of Leonard Cohen. Managed by Maarten Massa. https://www.maartenmassa.be/CohenChords/.
Leonard Cohen Official Site. http://www.leonardcohen.com/us/home.

# The Work of Leonard Cohen Referred to or Quoted

## BOOKS (IN ORDER OF PUBLICATION)

*Let Us Compare Mythologies*
    For Wilf and His House, 93
*The Spice-Box of Earth*, 1, 71
    After the Sabbath Prayers, 67
    Before the Story, 40
    To a Teacher, 10
    I Have Not Lingered in European Monasteries, 7
    It Swings, Jocko, 83
    Brighter than Our Sun, 58
    Last Dance at the Four Penny, 10, 52
    Song for Abraham Klein, 20
    Summer Haiku, 63
    Priests 1957, 58
    Isaiah, 72
    Lines from My Grandfather's Journal, 6, 52
*The Favourite Game*, 52, 58
    Book II, Chapter 12, 26, 57
    Book IV, Chapter 15, 6
*Beautiful Losers*, 57

*Death of a Lady's Man*, 13
    Formal in his Thought of Her, 63
    The End of My Life in Art, 25–26
*Stranger Music—Selected Poems and Songs*, 1, 56
    Roshi, 63
    Roshi again, 25–26
*Book of Longing*, 1, 9
    Roshi At 89, 19
    One of My Letters, 64
    You'd Sing Too 22
    Roshi, 63–64
    Dear Roshi, 49
    Leaving Mt. Baldy
    Moving Into A Period, 37–38, 79, 96
    *just to have been one of them*, 78
    You Are Right, Sahara, 28
    Why I Love France, 51, 93
    Puppets, 96
    Gravity , 212

# The Work of Leonard Cohen Referred to or Quoted

## ALBUMS AND SONGS (IN ORDER OF RELEASE)

*Songs of Leonard Cohen*
  Suzanne, 44, 59
  Master Song, 23–24
  The Stranger Song, 26, 56
  Sisters Of Mercy, 9, 28, 44
  So Long Marianne, 66
  Stories Of The Street, 61, 82
  Teachers, 11, 54
*Songs from a Room*
  Bird On A Wire, 61
  Story Of Isaac, 33, 45, 75
  The Old Revolution, 86
*Songs of Love and Hate*
  Last Year's Man, 48
  Joan Of Arc, 56
*Live Songs*
  Please Don't Pass Me By (A Disgrace), 66
*New Skin for the Old Ceremony*
  Lover, Lover, Lover, 30, 91
  A Singer Must Die, 22
*Death of a Ladies' Man*
  Fingerprints, 45
*Recent Songs*
  The Window, 4n, 78n
  Our Lady Of Solitude, 56
  The Gypsy's Wife, 66
*Various Positions*
  Dance Me to the End of Love, 50, 51, 61
  Coming Back to You, 86, 109
  The Law, 40, 42, 79
  Night Comes On, 37, 44, 63
  Hallelujah, 19, 32, 40, 62, 88, 93, 107
  The Captain, 61
  Hunter's Lullaby, 86–87
  Heart With No Companion, 98
  If It Be Your Will, 31–33, 56
*I'm Your Man*
  Take This Waltz, 66
  Tower Of Song, 22, 86
*The Future*
  The Future, 75, 109
  Waiting For The Miracle, 106–7
  Anthem, 75, 105–6
  Democracy, 75
*Ten New Songs*
  Here It Is, 91
  Boogie Street, 47, 91
*Dear Heather*
  Villanelle For Our Time, 11
  To A Teacher, 10
*Old Ideas*
  Going Home, 23
  Amen, 20
  Show Me The Place, 43, 105
  Darkness, 105
  Come Healing, 35
*Popular Problems*
  Almost Like the Blues, 66
  Born in Chains, 104
*You Want It Darker*
  You Want It Darker, 102
  Treaty, 3
*Thanks for the Dance*
  The Night Of Santiago, 66
  It's Torn, 38
  Puppets, 96

# Ancient Document Index

## THE HEBREW BIBLE

### Genesis

| | |
|---|---|
| 1 | 55 |
| 1:1 | 46 |
| 1:5 | 47 |
| 2:1 | 81 |
| 2:7 | 38, 53, 78 |
| 2:18 | 58 |
| 2-3 | 31 |
| 3:21 | 33 |
| 3:24 | 55 |
| 9 | 71 |
| 9:1-17 | 76 |
| 10 | 85 |
| 11:7-9 | 62 |
| 15:1 | 62 |
| 16 | 54 |
| 17 | 48, 54 |
| 21 | 54 |
| 22 | 33, 45, 65 |
| 28:12 | 78 |
| 28:18 | 34 |
| 32 | 108 |
| 32:24-25 | 47 |
| 32:24-32 | 76 |
| 32-33 | 47 |
| 33:4 | 47 |

### Exodus

| | |
|---|---|
| 32:15-16 | 52-53 |
| 33:13 | 77 |
| 34:6-7 | 89 |

### Leviticus

| | |
|---|---|
| 19:9-10 | 67 |
| 23:22 | 67 |
| 25:8-17 | 3 |
| 25:4-5 | 51 |
| 25:23 | 75 |

### Deuteronomy

| | |
|---|---|
| 10:16 | 48 |
| 11:17 | 84 |
| 11:18 | 55 |
| 11:20 | 55 |
| 28 | 75 |
| 30:19 | 30, 80 |
| 32:8 | 75 |

### 1 Samuel

| | |
|---|---|
| 24 | 59 |
| 25:17 | 107 |
| 30:22 | 107 |

# Ancient Document Index

## 2 Samuel
| | |
|---|---|
| 3:39 | 107 |
| 6:14–23 | 73 |
| 12:13 | 39 |
| 20:1 | 107 |

## 1 Kings
| | |
|---|---|
| 19 | 99 |

## 2 Kings
| | |
|---|---|
| 2:11–12 | 102 |

## Isaiah
| | |
|---|---|
| 1:7 | 72 |
| 6:1–2 | 78 |
| 6:3 | 6, 21, 94, 101 |
| 14:12 | 42 |
| 13–23 | 75 |
| 41:18 | 33 |
| 45:7 | 80 |
| 66:1 | 81 |

## Jeremiah
| | |
|---|---|
| 2:2 | 84 |

## Ezekiel
| | |
|---|---|
| 1 | 102 |
| 25–36 | 75 |
| 36:26 | 68 |
| 37:1–14 | 50 |

## Hosea
| | |
|---|---|
| 12:5 | 76 |

## Amos
| | |
|---|---|
| 1–2 | 75 |
| 9:13 | 33 |

## Zechariah
| | |
|---|---|
| 14:9 | 62 |

## Psalms
| | |
|---|---|
| 13:2–3 | 41 |
| 18:5–7 | 50 |
| 23:4 | 87, 89 |
| 23:6 | 78, 85 |
| 25:4 | 77 |
| 27:11 | 77 |
| 40:5 | 35 |
| 42:10 | 62 |
| 51:6 | 39–40 |
| 51:17 | 41 |
| 65:13 | 33 |
| 67:5 | 72 |
| 86:15 | 89 |
| 91:1–3 | 99 |
| 91:2, 5 | 84 |
| 100:2 | 97 |
| 103:8 | 89 |
| 103:15–16 | 88 |
| 103:19 | 81 |
| 103–4 | 78 |
| 106:2 | 47 |
| 116:7 | 57 |
| 119:33 | 85 |
| 119:103 | 45 |
| 121:6 | 53 |
| 132:7 | 81 |
| 136:8–9 | 53 |
| 139:7–10 | 50 |
| 145:14 | 42 |
| 146:3 | 35 |
| 150:1–4 | 81 |

## Proverbs
| | |
|---|---|
| 10:28 | 77 |

## Job
| | |
|---|---|
| 1 | 91 |
| 4:18 | 35 |
| 7:1–2, 9–10 | 88 |

## Song of Songs
| | |
|---|---|
| | 81 |

# Ancient Document Index

## Lamentations

| | |
|---|---|
| 3:24 | 103 |

## 1 Chronicles

| | |
|---|---|
| 28:2 | 81 |

## THE NEW TESTAMENT

### Matthew

| | |
|---|---|
| 15:24 | 82 |
| 27:50–53 | 32 |

### Luke

| | |
|---|---|
| 10 | 85 |
| 22:42 | 32 |

### John

| | |
|---|---|
| 1:1–5 | 55 |
| 19:30 | 81 |

## MISHNAH

### Avot

| | |
|---|---|
| 1:1 | 64 |
| 1:6 | 27 |
| 3:13 | 64 |
| 3:15 | 80 |

### Yoma

| | |
|---|---|
| | 38 |

## BABYLONIAN TALMUD

| | |
|---|---|
| Berachot 17a | 36 |
| Berachot 32b | 35 |
| Shabbat 33b | 70 |
| Taanit 23a | 27 |
| Moed Katan 24a | 54 |
| Nedarim 50a | 71 |
| Sanhedrin 44a | 71–72 |
| Bava Metzia 84a | 27 |
| Bava Batra 16a | 100 |
| Sanhedrin | 103 |

## MIDRASH

### Bereshit Rabba

| | |
|---|---|
| 3:7 | 68 |
| 8:1 | 92 |
| 10:6 | 79 |
| 17:3 | 58 |
| 20:12 | 33 |

### Midrash Tehilim

| | |
|---|---|
| 4:3 | 35 |

### Qohelet Rabbah

| | |
|---|---|
| 1:2 | 95 |

## SIDDUR / JEWISH PRAYER BOOK

| | |
|---|---|
| 'Amidah | 41, 42, 43, 62, 83, 108 |
| 'Arvit | 49 |
| Berachot | 83 |
| Birchot ha-Shachar | 98 |
| Birkat Kohanim | 82 |
| Havdalah | 71 |
| Kaddish | 44, 102 |
| Kiddush | 94 |
| Keter Malchut | 47–48 |
| Kri'at Shem'a 'al ha-Mitah | 94 |
| Ma'oz Tzur | 101 |
| Musaf | 21 |
| Pittum ha-Ktoret | 90 |
| Seder ha-'Avodah | 38 |
| Selichot | 20, 89 |

## ANCIENT DOCUMENT INDEX

### SIDDUR / JEWISH PRAYER BOOK (*cont.*)

| | |
|---|---|
| *Shem'a* | 21, 39, 77, 78, 107 |
| *Tikkun Chatzot* | 71 |
| *Viddui* | 80 |
| *Yedid Nefesh* | 108 |
| *Yigdal* | 62 |

### SEFER HA-ZOHAR / BOOK OF SPLENDOR

| | |
|---|---|
| I, 15a | 46 |
| I, 32a | 46 |
| I, 34b | 92 |
| I, 36b | 34 |
| I, 224b | 36–37 |
| II, 99a | 26 |
| III, 8ab | 97 |
| *Tikkunei Zohar* 57 | 94–95 |

# Subject Index

*Book of Visions, The*, 102–3
Buddhism and/or Zen, 2, 5, 7, 8, 9,
    10, 12, 17, 18, 19, 20, 22, 24,
    25, 26, 27, 28, 32, 39, 41, 46,
    49, 59, 62, 63, 64, 65, 67, 85,
    90, 102, 103, 107

Christianity, 41, 42, 45, 49, 55, 66

Daoism, 108
Dead Sea Scrolls, 29
Depression, 3, 8, 23, 61, 67, 95

Eden, 31, 37, 42, 55

Hasidism, 1, 2, 18, 93, 96, 101
  'Avodah be-Gashmi'yut, 101
  *Devekut*, 96, 107
  Sayings of Menachem Mendel,
    the Rabbi of Kotzk, 93, 95,
    96, 99
  Sayings of Rabbi Nachman of
    Bratslav, *hitbodedut*, 98, 100
Holocaust, the, 50, 61, 66, 69, 85

*I Ching* or *Classic of Changes*, 106

Jubilee, 3, 51

Kabbalah, 1, 2, 4, 8, 10, 13, 17, 18,
    19, 20, 30, 34, 68, 69, 70,
    71, 79, 80, 82, 84, 96, 101,
    102, 103

Lurianic Kabbalah, 13, 18, 69, 80,
    84, 101, 103

Merkavah Mysticism, 102

*Responsa from Heaven*, 102
Romans, 60, 70, 71

*Sefer Yetzirah* (Book of Creation), 9
*Sefirot* (from to to bottom), 10, 17,
    18, 21, 36, 38, 43, 48, 51, 53,
    54, 56, 89, 92, 107
  *Keter* (Crown; Will), 30, 36, 38,
    46, 47, 91, 107
  *Chochmah* (Wisdom; Higher
    Father), 36, 54, 107
  *Binah*, (Understanding; Higher
    Mother) 36, 54, 56, 107
  *Chesed* (Grace; Love; Abraham),
    81, 89
  *Gevurah* (Severity; Judgment;
    Isaac), 89, 105
  *Tif'eret* (Beauty; Mercy; Sun;
    Jacob; male), 10, 17, 89

## Subject Index

*Sefirot (cont.)*
   *Netzach* (Eternity; Endurance), 81
   *Hod* (Splendor), 57
   *Yesod* (Foundation; Rightous one), 43
   *Malchut* (Kingdom; *Shechinah*-Presence; moon; David; female) 10, 17, 36, 37, 38, 48, 49, 53, 69, 89, 90, 96

Seven Laws of Noah, 71, 76

# Places Index

Berlin, 76

Canada, ix, 7, 26, 69

France, ix, 3, 51, 59, 60, 93

Israel, 30, 58, 75, 76, 82, 84

Jerusalem, ix, 17, 20, 35, 37, 38, 65, 71, 72, 81, 84, 90, 96

Linz, 32

Los Angeles, 5, 67, 111

Montreal, 4, 5, 10, 35, 52, 59, 67

Mount Baldy, 5, 32

Moscow, 72

New York, 30, 67

Provence, 3, 51, 93

Ramat Gan, 82

Sinai, 30, 44, 52, 58

Spain, 17, 47, 66, 70

Tel Aviv, 58

Warsaw, 41

Washington, 72

# Names Index

Azikri, Elazar, 108
Akutagawa, Ryūnosuke, 59
Aristotel, 51

Balsekar, Ramesh S., 5, 8
Bodhidharma, 24

Caspi, Matti, 58
Cohen, Adam, 3, 31
Cohen, Lorca, 3
Cohen, Masha, 69

Dazu Huike, 24

Elrod, Suzanne, 3, 51
Elsen, Michael van, 9

Ibn Gabirol, Solomon, 47–48
Ihlen, Marianne, 74

Klein, Abraham M., 11
Klonitzki-Kline, Solomon, 4, 52

Layton, Irving, 11, 52
Lorca, Federico Garcia, 65, 66
Luria, Isaac, 18

Menachem Mendel of Kotzk, 93, 95, 96, 99
Milton, John, 108–9

Nachman of Bratslav, 98, 100

Plato, 92

Rembrandt, 76
Rosengarten, Mort, 52
Roshi (Joshu Sasaki), 5, 8, 10, 19, 25, 26, 37, 49, 54, 62, 63, 65, 93

Simon, Paul, 69
Scott, F. R., 10, 11
Shelley, Percy Bysshe, 57
St. John of the Cross, 34

Vital, Haim, 103

Wolfson, Elliot R., 4, 18

Yeats, William Butler, 73
Yitzhaki, Shlomo (Rashi), 93

Zach, Nathan, 58

# A List of Key Words in the Book

*References are to one of the main places where each word is discussed, usually mentioning the number of times it appears in the book*

Bind, 45
Blessed, 98
Bride, 69
Broken, 46

Dance, 72–73
Darkness, 85
Dew, 83

Exile, 68–69

Fall, 42–43
Family, 49
Foundation, 43

God, 73

Heart, 98

Joy, 61

Law, 40
Light, 85

Loneliness, 43
Longing, 77
Love, 81

Mercy, 20

Name, 43

Place, 43

Shelter, 99
Shield, 30
Solitude, 43

Table, 100
Teacher, 62–63
Tears, 52
Throne, 91

Unity, 62

Will, 28–30

www.ingramcontent.com/pod-product-compliance
Lightning Source LLC
Chambersburg PA
CBHW071623170426
43195CB00038B/2041